INTRODUCTION

We live an individualistic society. Everything is personalized. Coke *cans* have our names on them. Coke *machines* provide literally thousands of mix-and-match options. Even music providers cater to individuals: a Pandora commercial boasts that "your thumb is the DJ."

It's no wonder that this rugged individualism has crept into the church, or even made professing Christians creep *out of* the church. Even Christians are prone to think in terms of "me." But the New Testament unmistakably and unabashedly speaks in terms of "us." Most of the New Testament was written *to* local churches or their leaders. Much of it is written *about* local churches. When Christ restores the fallen Peter, he tells him three times that he will prove his love for Jesus by caring for Jesus' flock. And when Christ lays out his plan for the ages, he says, "I will build my church." When Acts records the spread of Christianity throughout Asia and Europe, it records the planting of local churches. When sinners become saints, they invariably are baptized and connected to local churches. Even the magnificent book of Revelation was written to seven local churches. The church matters. To quote the carefully chosen name of the company that publishes this book, the "Church Works!"

Motivated by a deep love for Christ's church—flawed as it is on this side of heaven—it is our pleasure to provide thirty-one devotional lessons that focus on the nature, mission, and corporate life of the local church. The book's target audience isn't leaders, but entire congregations. Each devotional seeks to connect the life-giving truth of the gospel with life-shaping applications for the congregation. We're praying that the Lord will use these lessons to increase the love of Christians for both our Savior and his church. Read them with an open Bible and an open heart, praying that the Lord will work in your life and in your church. That's a prayer he will surely answer, for his glory!

Chris Anderson for Joe Tyrpak and Dave Doran

Dedicated to the members of Inter-City Baptist Church, Killian Hill Baptist Church, and Tri-County Bible Church, our "joy and crown" (Philippians 4:1). May Christ continue to build his church as we labor together with you!

Kudos to Dan Totten for his exceptional editing. Thank you for partnering with us in this endeavor.

© 2015 by churchworksmedia.com. All rights reserved.

Scripture quotations are from *The Holy Bible, English Standard Version*, copyright © 2001 by Crossway Bibles, a division of Good News Publishers. Used by permission. All rights reserved.

DAY 1 — READ 1 TIMOTHY 3:14–4:16

THE CHURCH, A PILLAR AND BUTTRESS

"The church of the living God [is] a pillar and buttress of truth." 1 TIMOTHY 3:15

Did you know that gospel hymns were sung within a few decades of the historical events of the gospel? One such hymn is found in 1 Timothy 3:16. The brief chorus rehearses six historical realities of the gospel: Jesus' incarnation, resurrection, exaltation, worldwide proclamation and reception, and glorious ascension. What glorious truth! The eternal God became a man. He died but didn't stay dead. He rose again and now sits on a throne surrounded by angelic powers. The gospel is mightily advancing throughout the world as the enthroned Messiah always lives to pray for his people. That's truth that every Christian should confess, study, wonder at, sing, and live out. (Each of these responses is implied in 1 Timothy 3:16.)

God calls the church to be "a pillar and buttress" of that amazing truth. In using the imagery of pillars and buttresses, Paul is thinking of the church (as he often does) as God's temple. And even though it's a bit strange to speak of us supporting the gospel, Paul teaches that God has designed the church to uphold and promote the gospel like the temple pillars and buttresses upheld the roof and walls of that beautiful structure. How does a church exalt the gospel? In the verses that follow, Paul explains at least three ways in which churches (especially the leaders) lift high the gospel.

You lift high the gospel when you receive God's gifts with thankful enjoyment (4:1–5). False religion was rampant in Paul's day, and it's rampant in ours. When Paul warns Timothy about demonic deception from those with seared consciences, you might think he's referring to occultic witches. Instead, the demonic, deceptive teaching he's concerned about is this: required celibacy for church leaders and required abstinence from certain foods. That demonism describes most of professing Christendom today! Paul teaches that godliness is not marked by ascetic, man-made rules, but by biblically enjoying God's blessings with thankfulness (vv. 3–4). As simple as it seems, if you receive God's good gifts—everyday gifts like lunch and marital sexuality—with thankful enjoyment, you'll lift high the gospel. You'll show that the gospel has transformed you to live human life as God intended it: with God (not his gifts) at the center.

You lift high the gospel when you pursue godliness with toilsome exercise (4:6–10). The antidote to man-made religion is a regular training regimen in good doctrine. Paul commands Timothy, "Train yourself for godliness" (v. 7). He says that everyone should agree with the conviction that bodily exercise has value for this life, but godliness has value for both this life and the next (vv. 8–9). A disciplined pursuit of growth in doctrinal understanding is crucial not only for pastors. It's for every believer. You will not grow as a Christian, a Christian evangelist, a Christian husband or wife, or a Christian parent if you're not toiling and striving to better understand what God's Word teaches. Those who consistently pursue a fuller apprehension of God's will for their lives exalt the life-changing truth of the gospel.

You lift high the gospel when you teach God's Word with a transparent example (4:11–16). Paul was concerned that Pastor Timothy give himself to reading Scripture publicly, making practical application of it, and providing doctrinal instruction (v. 13). But Paul was concerned with more than what Timothy taught. He was also concerned with how Timothy's teaching was backed up by his life. If you regularly teach the Word, you must carefully watch your words, actions, love, and purity (v. 12). The Lord doesn't expect you to be a perfect Christian, just a *pattern* Christian. He doesn't expect you to be an extraordinary Christian, just an *ordinary* one. You will lift high the gospel by living an unhypocritical life, being careful to walk what you talk. And remember, the "only thing" that's at stake in lifting high the gospel is people's salvation (v. 16).

Let the advancement of the gospel fuel your thankfulness, toil, and transparency. —JOE

DAY 2 — READ COLOSSIANS 3

WORD-FILLED CHURCHES SING!

"Let the word of Christ dwell in you richly, teaching and . . . singing." COLOSSIANS 3:16

Colossians 3:16 commands the church to make the Bible lavishly at home in our hearts. A healthy church is so saturated with the Scriptures that the Word overflows in corporate communication: in teaching each other and in singing to the Lord. Because I love to sing, especially with my local church, I want to focus on the latter.

Congregational singing should be saturated with Scripture. The Bible doesn't allow the church to sing whatever it wants. It tells us to sing the Word. We are to meditate deeply on the Bible, and that meditation is to seep into our songs—both those we choose and those we compose. We should insist on songs that have overt Biblical concepts, quotations, and allusions. Sure, our lyrics should be artistic and emotive, not banal rhymes that inspire neither mind nor heart. But they must always, *always* be Biblical. In fact, some should be more than Biblical—they should be *Bible*. Sing the Psalms! Whether old or new, our songs should be vehicles that carry to our hearts and from our lips the very Word of God.

Congregational singing should make much of Christ. It is significant that the Bible is described in Colossians 3:16 as "the word of Christ." It's not just a collection of truths about God and his people, occasionally mentioning Christ. Both Testaments focus on Christ as the Savior of fallen humanity. Even "psalms" are categorized by Paul under the heading "the word of Christ." All Scripture points to Christ, but the Bible's Christ-centeredness crescendos to a *fortissimo* in the book of Colossians. Paul urges Christians not to turn aside from Christ to philosophy, tradition, mysticism, or ascetic regulations (2:8, 16–23). He tells us that Jesus is the exact representation of the invisible God, the Creator and Sustainer of all things, the only Savior from sin, the Head of the church, and the Reconciler of all things to God (1:13–23). After all this doctrine—some of the most stirring in all the Bible—Paul tells us that Christ should fill our *songs*. Jesus is both the *subject* of our songs (we sing "the word of Christ") and the *object* of our songs (we sing "to the Lord"). Here's a good rule of thumb: If an Orthodox Jew, a Mormon, or a Jehovah's Witness could sing most of our songs with hearty agreement, we're probably singing the wrong songs.

Congregational singing should overflow from joyful hearts. Our text began by describing the gospel's dwelling "in" us, and it concludes by teaching that our songs should be the expression of "grace in [our] hearts." As important as text and tune are, they're pointless if they don't come from hearts transformed by God's grace. True worship doesn't start with well-rehearsed choirs and loud singing; it begins with congregants who are mindful of God's grace extended to them through the gospel of Jesus Christ. That's why Paul in Ephesians 5:18–19—the other "psalms and hymns and spiritual songs" text—insists that our songs flow out of hearts that are filled with the *Spirit* in addition to being filled with the *Scriptures*. Praise is a spiritual, grace-enabled exercise.

Music is a wonderful thing. It allows us to combine our voices in beautiful and unified praise. And it's a powerful thing—it both *reflects* and *shapes* church doctrine, perhaps as much or more than sermons! I value preaching as a God-ordained means of grace. But the reality is that songs often stay with us long after sermons are forgotten. Think of it this way: How many of John Wesley's sermons can you quote? Probably none. But you can almost surely recite several of the hymns written by his brother Charles, like "And Can It Be," "O for a Thousand Tongues to Sing," and "Hark the Herald Angels Sing." Hymns stick, so let's use them well. May our churches be *Bible-fed* and *Spirit-led*, and may our songs and singing show it!

Let the gospel so thrill your heart that it overflows in Christ-saturated singing.—CHRIS

DAY 3 — READ 2 TIMOTHY 3

THE POWER OF GODLINESS

"Having the appearance of godliness, but denying its power. Avoid such people." 2 TIMOTHY 3:5

Although this verse directly addresses false teachers, it also reveals a profound truth about the difference between false and genuine Christianity. When Paul says that the false teachers hold to "the appearance of godliness" that denies "its power," he opens our eyes to see both the danger of formal religion and the power of genuine godliness. It is very possible to be religious without being regenerate. It is possible to adopt a form of Christianity without having the substance of it.

This text asserts that genuine godliness has power. The implication of the text, in light of its context, is that the power of godliness changes a believer so that he or she is different from the characteristics that Paul enumerates:

> For people will be lovers of self, lovers of money, proud, arrogant, abusive, disobedient to their parents, ungrateful, unholy, heartless, unappeasable, slanderous, without self-control, brutal, not loving good, treacherous, reckless, swollen with conceit, lovers of pleasure rather than lovers of God (3:2–4).

Remember, these characteristics belong to people who have "the appearance of godliness." It is only appearance because true godliness contradicts these characteristics.

The degeneration that Paul warned about is counteracted by the power of regeneration. To be religious without a radical break from the course and conduct of the world is to hold a form of godliness that denies its power. Genuine Christianity is never less than sound doctrine but is always more than doctrine alone. A creed without transformed conduct is something different and something less than genuine Christianity. That's because genuine Christianity is built on the power of God through the gospel and is displayed in the power of godliness that transforms sinners into Christlikeness. This should not surprise us. The God we worship is the living God, not the dead idols of pagan rituals or the empty ideas of pagan philosophy. We serve a God who hears and acts on behalf of those who wait for him (Isaiah 64:4). We have been saved by a God who, by his Spirit, strengthens us with power in the inner person (Ephesians 3:16–17) and who works in the saved both "to will and to work for his good pleasure" (Philippians 2:13).

Lifeless and powerless Christianity is not Biblical Christianity. The bizarre beliefs and practices of some segments of professing Christendom must be rejected, but we must be careful not allow our desire for genuine spiritual power to be too shallow. The fact that some abuse the concept of spiritual power is no reason for us ignore it. Without spiritual power, genuine Christian experience is impossible—we must have the power of the gospel and the dynamic work of the Spirit!

If our Christianity is powerless, then it is not real. If our Christianity is real, then God's power is operating in our lives and congregations. Gospel-believing churches should be places where God's power is evident in the conversion of sinners, the transformation of believers, and the fulfillment of the Great Commission. Let's not play Christianity; let's really live it!

The Apostle Paul prayed specifically for the believers in Ephesus to understand and experience the resurrection power of God in their lives (Ephesians 1:19–20). Will you pray for that in your own life? Will you intercede for your believing family and friends to be "strengthened with power through his Spirit" (Ephesians 3:16)? Will you pray that the proclamation of the gospel from your church is "not only in word, but also in power and in the Holy Spirit and with full conviction" (1 Thessalonians 1:5)? May God graciously pour out fresh gospel power to transform our lives and magnify his mercy among the nations!

Let the gospel powerfully transform your life and church!—DAVE

DAY 4 — READ LUKE 19:1–10

MISSIONS ONE BY ONE

"The Son of Man came to seek and to save the lost." LUKE 19:10

Do you believe that people can really change? Many don't think it's possible. But Zacchaeus' life stands as a testimony to Jesus' power to change lives. When the account opens, Zacchaeus is a rich, notoriously deceptive and money-hungry tax collector who wants to catch a glimpse of Jesus. When the account ends, Zacchaeus, because of his encounter with Jesus, is joyful, honest, and generous—a changed man at the core. Zacchaeus' greed gave way to generosity. His secrecy and deception gave way to a transparent confession of Jesus as his Lord. So can people really change? The answer of this passage is *yes*. How does it happen? The brief account provides at least three answers.

Life change is made possible by Jesus' trip to Jerusalem (v. 1). It's significant that Jesus was only "passing through" Jericho on his way to Jerusalem. For ten chapters Luke has been emphasizing Jerusalem as Jesus' target destination (see Luke 9:51; 13:22; 17:11). In Jerusalem "everything that is written about the Son of Man by the prophets will be accomplished. . . . He will be delivered over to the Gentiles and will be mocked. . . . After flogging him, they will kill him, and on the third day he will rise" (18:31–33). The gospel—the good news of what Jesus accomplished at Jerusalem—makes life change possible. Change in Zacchaeus didn't work like a diet in which willpower exerted over time gradually leads to noticeable change. Instead, life change is made possible when you personally encounter the historical Jesus who died and rose again in Jerusalem.

Total life change is possible for the most despised and disadvantaged (vv. 2-4). Zacchaeus wanted to get a glimpse of the famed evangelist but had several things working against him: he was a tax collector, he was wealthy, he was short, and he was just one individual in a vast crowd. Because of these disadvantages "he could not" see Jesus (v. 3). Luke's account of the gospel emphasizes Jesus' special interest in the rejects of society—in unclean shepherds, helpless widows, barren women, ignored children, overlooked beggars, hated Samaritans, possessed lunatics, notorious prostitutes, untouchable lepers, and ostracized tax collectors. So Zacchaeus is typical of the people that Jesus came to seek and save. The fact that he was despised and disadvantaged meant he was the target of Jesus' saving mission. Because they misunderstand Jesus' mission, many Christians try to hide the problems and shame of their past. How sad! Don't act like your past never happened. Instead, frankly rehearse the disadvantages of your past in order to highlight Jesus' remarkable mercy to you.

Change occurs when you respond to Jesus' invitation (vv. 5-7). Jesus could've walked past Zacchaeus, but he didn't. Although he had no obligation to love this sinful man, Jesus invited himself to Zacchaeus' house saying, "Today in your house I *must* come to stay" (my translation). Jesus choice to love Zacchaeus was scandalous. The crowds hated him for doing so (see also Luke 5:30; 7:39; 15:2). When Jesus invited himself, Zacchaeus immediately responded: He gladly took Jesus to his house. And that was the last time anyone saw the old Zacchaeus. Change occurs when you encounter Jesus, hear his personal invitation to you, and gladly welcome him.

Churches are most Christlike when we seek the conversion of one disadvantaged sinner at a time. One-at-a-time evangelism is an approach that's often belittled today by Christians who imagine the church's mission to be much bigger. But what kind of evangelistic strategy makes the biggest difference? Sociologist Robert Woodberry researched for more than a decade to determine what makes third world countries develop. He concluded:

> Areas where [nineteenth-century conversionary] Protestant missionaries had a significant presence in the past are on average more economically developed today, with comparatively better health, lower infant mortality, lower corruption, greater literacy, [and] higher educational attainment (especially for women)" (*Christianity Today*, January/February 2014, pp. 39–40).

How do churches today seek the good of entire cultures? By preaching the gospel to sinners, one Zacchaeus at a time.

Trust the gospel to bring remarkable change, one disadvantaged sinner at a time.—JOE

DAY 5 — READ 1 CORINTHIANS 3

DON'T MESS WITH CHRIST'S CHURCH

"If anyone destroys God's temple, God will destroy him." 1 CORINTHIANS 3:17

We are far too cavalier about criticizing churches, whether our own or the church down the street. In some circles, it's actually a mark of spiritual discernment to uncork on the "compromising" church across town, even if it's a gospel preaching church. I'll never forget witnessing an example of this about a decade ago. The church I pastored had a makeshift "float" in a community parade. We wore t-shirts to identify ourselves and distributed literature to invite people to visit our services. Another church—a more contemporary church—was doing the same thing, but their float was a stage for their church's praise band. Their music had a serious "thump" to it; ours didn't. We had some notable differences, but we both preached the gospel. I was heartsick to see the disgust—indeed, the hatred—on the face of one of our church members as he glared at them across the parking lot. Is such antipathy justified? Perhaps if the church is really flawed? I believe the answer from 1 Corinthians 3:16–17 is *no*.

Even flawed churches that preach the gospel are God's temple (v. 16). The local church at Corinth was famously flawed. Paul called their behavior "fleshly" (3:1–3). He reprimanded them for divisiveness (1:10–17; 3:4), tolerance of gross immorality (5:1–2), lawsuits against fellow Christians (6:1–8), abuse of spiritual gifts (Chapters 12–14), and other church problems. And yet, Paul referred to them as "saints" who have been "sanctified" (1:1–2). And in 3:16, he referred to them collectively as the temple of God. In the Old Testament, God uniquely resided in the tabernacle and temple. But since Pentecost, God has lived within his people as his *living* temple (1 Peter 2:5). Even the miraculous symbols in the upper room in Acts 2 highlight the fact that God's new residence is his people, not a building. (See *Gospel Meditations for Missions*, Day 16.) God lives in individual Christians (1 Corinthians 6:19–20). But he also lives in us collectively—the local church is his temple (1 Corinthians 3:16–17). That's why the pronouns in 3:16–17 are plural in the original Greek: "You [plural, as a group] are God's temple and . . . God's Spirit dwells in you [plural, as a group]." Bottom line: The church—even a church with as many problems as the church at Corinth—is God's temple.

God will "destroy" those who harm His temple—the local church (v. 17). First Corinthians 3:16 is inspiring. But 1 Corinthians 3:17 is frightening. God will destroy those who destroy his temple. Here's the imagery: Think of how protective God was of the Old Testament temple. Only believers could enter—and only after going through symbolic purifications and sacrifices. Beyond that, only priests could access the Holy Place. Entrance into the Holy of Holies was even more exclusive: Only the high priest could pass beyond the veil—and that only once per year, on the Day of Atonement. When people defiled the temple, they died. Think of Hophni and Phineas (1 Samuel 2:12–17, 22–26, 34; 4:11). Can you imagine rushing into God's temple and defacing it, say through graffiti or vandalism? Only if you had a death wish! But Paul says that those who harm the local church are actually defacing God's temple—and God will *destroy* them! This is vitally important. The whole point of Chapter 3 is to reprove division in the church. Paul argues for unity from a variety of angles, but his climactic argument is that the church—even a church like Corinth—is God's temple, and therefore God will destroy those who harm it.

What does that mean to us today? We should value the church, imperfect as it is. And we should fear raising a finger—or a voice—against it. To put it bluntly: *Don't mess with Christ's church!*

Let the gospel instill in you a holy protectiveness for gospel-preaching churches.—CHRIS

DAY 6 — READ ACTS 14:24–15:14

GOD'S COWORKERS

"And all the assembly fell silent, and they listened to Barnabas and Paul as they related what signs and wonders God had done through them among the Gentiles." ACTS 15:12

Acts 15:12 speaks about God's work in the Gentile mission, and it shows how closely God's work is tied to that of his servants ("what…God had done through them"). It actually is the third time Luke communicates this idea. Look at two verses from earlier in the passage:

> And when they arrived and gathered the church together, they declared all that God had done with them, and how he had opened a door of faith to the Gentiles (Acts 14:27).

> When they came to Jerusalem, they were welcomed by the church and the apostles and the elders, and they declared all that God had done with them (Acts 15:4).

So Barnabus and Paul "related what . . . God had done *through* them," and "they declared all that God had done *with* them." We probably should not make too much out of the preposition change from "through" to "with" since all three texts address the same subject for the same purpose. The change of preposition does not substantively change the meaning of the respective phrases.

That is not to say, however, that the phrases are not filled with wonderful truth and profound significance for God's people. In an amazing way, God condescends to become a coworker with his people—he is at work at the same time and in the same tasks as we are. That is why Paul can describe Timothy with the incredible words "our brother and God's coworker in the gospel of Christ" (1 Thessalonians 3:2). God's coworker! Amazing grace!

Obviously, God is not a coworker in any way that comes close to a co-equal partnership with his people in the work. These texts make that clear. In each verse the clear focus is on the words "what God had done." Paul and Barnabas were not bragging about what they had done, but exalting God for what he had done.

Having laid this foundation, let's state this wonderful concept in the form of three principles:

1. If anything of eternal significance is done, it is God who does it!

2. As an amazing display of his grace, the God who is not served by human hands (Acts 17:25) has chosen to allow his redeemed creatures to work with him to accomplish his purposes.

3. Even though we are privileged to be coworkers with God, the power and effectiveness of our work is not rooted in us but in the fact that God works through us. He is the source and strength of the work. We serve as conduits of his power.

I believe that God has arranged his economy in this way so that the historical circumstances of these verses will be repeated again and again throughout time and eternity—God's people gather to declare his glory by recounting what God has done. What a wonderful privilege to be involved in God's work, to have God working with and through us to accomplish his purposes. May God instill a deep and fervent longing in our hearts to be used like this, and may he grant us the privilege of testifying about the wonderful things that he has done!

Let the gospel privilege of being God's servant fill your heart with praise and godly ambition to be an instrument that he uses to do great things for his glory! —DAVE

DAY 7 — READ ACTS 18

"STRENGTHENING THE CHURCHES"

"They returned . . . strengthening the souls of the disciples." ACTS 14:21–22

When I think of the Apostle Paul, I think of the consummate frontline missionary. He was perpetually burdened about "the lands beyond" (Romans 15:20–21 and 2 Corinthians 10:16). He had a holy dissatisfaction with the *status quo* and a holy ambition for gospel advance. But it might surprise you to see how much of his missionary effort focused not on the *planting* of new churches but the *strengthening* of existing churches. As I understand it, over half of Paul's mission endeavors focused on maturing churches and training leaders. (Try to find maps of his three missionary journeys to reference during this study.)

Nearly half of Paul's first missionary journey was spent strengthening existing churches. His first mission trip (with Barnabas) is recorded in Acts 13–14. The initial work of these model missionaries focused on evangelism and church planting. They labored in a relatively small region called Galatia (modern-day central Turkey). They took the gospel to key cities: Antioch in Pisidia (not to be confused with their home church in Antioch in Syria), Iconium, Derbe, and Lystra. Their preaching met with opposition—and success. Sinners were saved and organized into local churches. But their work wasn't done. On their way home Paul and Barnabus visited the new church plants, "strengthening the disciples" and "appoint[ing] elders" (14:21–23).

Nearly half of Paul's second missionary journey was spent strengthening existing churches. After their first mission trip, they returned to Antioch (14:24–28), then went to Jerusalem to defend their new converts against the legalistic Judaizers (Ch. 15). They then decided to take another mission trip, motivated first of all to "return and visit the brothers in every city where [they had] proclaimed the word of the Lord, and see how they are" (15:36). Their disagreement over coworker John Mark caused them to separate, so Paul went with Silas on his second mission trip, recorded in Acts 16–18. This time, they *started* the trip by returning to the churches planted on Paul's first trip (15:41). The rest of the trip saw the greatest geographical expansion of Paul's ministry. Forbidden by the Spirit from going into Asia Minor, Paul instead was called into Macedonia and Greece—taking the gospel into Europe for the first time. He was back in church planting mode, as sinners were saved and organized into local churches in Philippi, Thessalonica, Berea, Corinth, and Ephesus (back in Asia).

Essentially all of Paul's third missionary journey was spent strengthening existing churches. Paul put more miles on his sandals on his third mission trip than on the first two combined. I've been privileged to follow his steps through Turkey and Greece, and that rugged part of the world is exhausting in a car, not to mention on foot. But Paul, nearing sixty years of age, had another road trip in him, and it's recorded in Acts 18–20. Once again his itinerary took him to Derbe, Lystra, Iconium, and Antioch in Pisidia where he went about "strengthening all the disciples" (18:23). *Deja vu!* From there he went to Ephesus where he spent three very productive years strengthening the church (Ch. 19). Where would you expect him to go next? Back to Philippi, Thessalonica, Berea, and Corinth—where he gave the local churches "much encouragement" (20:2). Having arrived in Corinth (the southern-most city he visited in Greece), Paul decided it was time to head home. Rather than sailing to Asia as he had on his second journey, he retraced his steps by going north and returning yet *again* to Berea, Thessalonica, and Philippi. From there, he made a brief stop at Troas (perhaps the one evangelistic stop on the trip; 20:5) and Miletus (for the leadership seminar recorded in 20:17–38), and eventually home.

What's the point of this admittedly redundant geography lesson? This: Paul didn't do drive-by evangelism. Yes, he perpetually stretched for the unreached. But he spent at least half of his *missionary journeys* strengthening churches and training leaders. And he supplemented those face-to-face visits with the letters we now cherish. Church health matters—both abroad and at home!

Let the gospel make you passionate about the strength of the church and its leaders.—CHRIS

DAY 8 — READ 1 CORINTHIANS 15

THE FIRST DAY OF THE WEEK

"On the first day of every week, each of you is to put something aside and store it up, as he may prosper, so that there will be no collecting when I come." 1 CORINTHIANS 16:2

Do Sundays wear you out? Do you start Sundays in a frenzy and finish them exhausted? Do you feel that gathering with the church on Sunday is getting old? At times I (along with many other Christians I know) have almost dreaded Sundays as the most stressful day of the week. If you're tired of Sunday church gatherings or if you've decided to take a break from them for a season, what should you do to re-engage? Well, I could recommend some practical ways to prepare better on Saturday, and I could recommend that you be realistic in the number of ministry commitments you can handle; but maybe the most helpful thing I can recommend is that you look to Biblical truth to remind yourself why Christians have gathered, for two millennia now, on the first day of every week.

Christians gather together every Sunday as a rhythmic reminder of Jesus' victory over death. Each of the four gospel accounts stresses that the resurrection occurred on Sunday: "the first day of the week" (Matthew 28:1), "on the first day of the week" (Mark 16:2), "on the first day of the week" (Luke 24:1), and "on the first day of the week" (John 20:1, 19). It's clear from a few places in the New Testament that although the church met frequently during the week (Acts 2:36), gathering on the first day of the week was their inviolable tradition. When Paul instructed the church at Corinth how to give, he indicated that they were in the habit of meeting "on the first day of *every* week" (1 Corinthians 16:2, italics mine). At Troas, the church gathered together "on the first day of the week . . . to break bread" (Acts 20:7). A funny and memorable event happened at this gathering of the church in Troas: Paul preached until midnight, and Eutychus fell asleep (and out the window) during the long sermon. It seems that the early church usually met in the evening because in the Roman world Sunday was a workday for many people. And it seems that the church (at least the one in Corinth) regularly combined their weekly "coming together" in the evening with a potluck dinner and the Lord's Table (1 Corinthians 11:17ff). So the first generation of Jesus' disciples met "on the first day of every week," a day they called "the Lord's Day" (Revelation 1:10). On the first day they broke bread. On the first day they met to get the apostles' teaching. On the first day they pooled together their resources for benevolence and missions. Why *on the first day*? As a weekly tradition that reminded them of the central event of the good news: their Lord's victory over sin and death.

Have you lost sight of why, after two millennia, Jesus' disciples continue to gather *on the first day of every week*? Has the tradition lost its meaning for you? Then you should start by reminding yourself every Sunday why you're gathering *on the first day of the week*. Meeting together with the church, especially on Sunday, gives an implicit reminder of all that Jesus' resurrection means. Meeting on Sunday should remind you that you're forgiven. His resurrection proved that your sins had been paid for in full. Meeting on Sunday should remind you that you don't need to fear death. Jesus' resurrection demonstrated that he has the power over death and that very soon it will be said, "Death is swallowed up in victory" (1 Corinthians 15:54). Meeting on Sunday should remind you that no service for Jesus is futile. Since Jesus conquered sin and death, you should continually "abound" (1 Corinthians 15:58) in exultant praise and toilsome ministry for the Victor. Meeting on Sunday should remind you that you have authority to spread the gospel. Your authority has been conferred on you by the risen King who posesseses all authority in heaven and on earth. Gathering *on the first day of the week* is a pregnant tradition. As Don Whitney teaches, meeting with the church to worship the risen Lord Jesus Christ should be a Christian's "greatest privilege and most important responsibility on the Lord's Day" (*Simplify Your Spiritual Life*, p. 167). Don't just endure Sundays. Love them!

Let the gospel be the reason you gather with other disciples on the first day of every week.—JOE

DAY 9 — READ ACTS 1

THE POWER OF A PRAYING CHURCH

"All these with one accord were devoting themselves to prayer." ACTS 1:14

Modern churches—whether they are proudly conservative or boast that they aren't "churchy"—have inherited years of traditions, suppositions, and strategies. That's not always bad. But we need to be intentional, knowing *why* we do *what* we do. Sometimes the best way to be certain that we're on task is to compare ourselves to the early church. The book of Acts shows what church life looked like before the church was encumbered with two millennia of ecclesiastical baggage. The early church was vibrant specifically because it prayed, non-stop.

The early church prayed whenever it assembled. The prayer in Acts 1:14 was corporate, unified, and constant. The disciples were awaiting the coming of the Spirit, and they used their time wisely. Stuart Custer, one of my seminary professors, comments on this first prayer meeting in Acts: "This prayer is going to start a cycle that runs all through Acts: Prayer, Power, Proclamation, Persecution, more Prayer" (*Witness to Christ*, p. 9).

The early church prayed when it was persecuted. The same Sanhedrin that slew Jesus set their sights on the early church in Acts 4. They arrested them and threatened them. The church's kneejerk response to persecution was *prayer*—prayer for boldness, not for safety (4:23–31). Their prayer was mightily answered, and the persecution resulted in more disciples, not fewer. In Acts 7 the persecution escalated to another murder. Stephen spent his last breaths on earth imitating his Savior by praying for the very people who killed him (7:59–60). In Acts 12, when James was martyred and Peter arrested, the church responded again with prayer, and their prayers were miraculously—and surprisingly!—answered (12:12). Finally, Paul and Silas, though battered and bloodied, spent their night in a Philippian jail praying and singing (16:25), leading to the conversion of a jailer and his family. The point: when you pierce Christ's church, *prayers* pour out!

The church prayed for its leaders. Nothing is more vital to the health of a church than the selection of leaders. The early church was careful not to choose leaders prayerlessly. Rather, they asked the all-wise God to show whom *he* wanted to replace Judas (1:24). Similarly, in Acts 6, the selection of the first deacons was handled with prayer. The apostles called for deacons to serve the church with nominal tasks precisely so that the apostles (and now pastors) would be freed up to "devote [them]selves to prayer and to the ministry of the Word" (6:4). Note the two essential elements of pastoral leadership: prayer and preaching—in that order! Once the deacons were chosen, the apostles predictably prayed for them, laying hands on them as a symbolic recognition of God's calling and enablement (6:6, as in 14:23). The result of this prayer-saturated leadership was the advance of the gospel and the growth of the church (6:7).

The church prayed for gospel expansion. It's a good thing for churches to pray together for health needs, employment needs, and the like. Such requests usually dominate a church's prayer list and prayer meeting. That's okay. But no request should be offered as passionately or remembered as faithfully as the prayer for the conversion of the lost. The early church prayed on multiple occasions as it sent laborers into the harvest (13:1–3; 20:36; 21:5). Sometimes these prayer meetings were tearful as the church sent out beloved members to take the gospel to unreached places. Praise God for those with the courage and conviction to leave their home and church for the sake of Christ's name. Pray for them, as Paul urged in 2 Thessalonians 3:1–2. Pray for the advance of the gospel and for the protection of those who are its champions.

Most of the prayers we've addressed here came at a "crossroads" for the early church—the selection of leaders, the hardship of persecution, and the sending out of missionaries. But far more frequent were the everyday prayers that became the rhythm of church life (2:42; 3:1; 9:36–40; 10:9; 16:13, 16; 27:27–29; 28:7–8). The early church was a praying church—and therefore a powerful church. Their prayers showed their need for divine assistance. *Do ours?*

Let the gospel drive your church to its knees in fervent corporate prayer. —CHRIS

DAY 10 — READ JOHN 17:1-21 & 20:21-23

JESUS' MISSION AND OURS

"Peace be with you. As the Father has sent me, even so I am sending you." JOHN 20:21

The Gospels and Acts all contain commission texts—places where Jesus commissions his disciples to fulfill the mission he entrusts to them for the time after his departure. The shortest of them is found in the Gospel of John (20:21). Surprisingly, though, in the second half of the twentieth century this verse became a key text for redefining the mission of the church. The argument, based on the "As…so" of the text, was that whatever Jesus did is what the church is to do. In some ways, the difference was captured by the shift to talking about *mission* rather than *missions*. *Missions* had been historically (properly!) focused on preaching the gospel and planting churches.

Mission was broader than that. Since Jesus did things such as feeding the hungry and healing the sick, our mission should include humanitarian efforts like these. For some, the mission of Jesus (and therefore the church) is seen as being a subset of God's mission to redeem the creation, so they expand the church's mission to include creation care and restructuring the social order so that it operates more justly. The new view of *mission* places humanitarian efforts on an equal level with gospel proclamation and church planting. The new view of *mission* also argues that it is just as much the church's mission to seek the temporal welfare of its city as it is to pursue the eternal welfare of the people in its city. Both are the mission of the church and neither holds a priority over the other.

There are a number of significant flaws in this understanding of the commission text here in John's Gospel. Before we even look at the verse itself, we must recognize how clearly all of the other commission texts focus on the proclamation of the gospel—Matthew, Mark, and Luke (both in his Gospel and Acts) all clearly record the Lord's commissions in terms of gospel proclamation. To take this text in John and force the others to mean something other than what they clearly say is terribly misguided.

The focus of John 20:21 (and 17:18) is on the words "sent" and "sending." It isn't about how Jesus came or really even what Jesus did, but that Jesus was commissioned by his Father to do the Father's will and now the disciples are being commissioned by the Son to do the Son's will. The language of sending focuses on the responsibility of the sent one to do something on behalf of the sender. This is very clear in John 4:34 when Jesus says to the disciples, "My food is to do the will of him who sent me and to accomplish his work." The will and work of the Sender were the top priority of the Sent One. And when Jesus reaches the end of his earthly ministry, he can say, "I glorified you on earth, having accomplished the work that you gave me to do" (John 17:4).

So the real question isn't, "What did Jesus do?" It really is, "What did Jesus give us to do?" What is the work that Jesus commissioned his disciples to perform? The other commission texts clearly focus on making disciples, preaching the good news to every creature, proclaiming the forgiveness of sins in Jesus' name, and being witnesses for Jesus Christ. The Apostle Peter understood what Jesus told them to do: "He commanded us to preach to the people and to testify that he is the one appointed by God to be judge of the living and the dead" (Acts 10:42).

Jesus commanded us to preach to the people. We have been sent just as he was sent. He finished his work—will we?

Let the gospel of God's grace through Jesus Christ propel you to fulfill the mission which we have been given by our Savior: to make disciples of all the nations!—DAVE

DAY 11 — READ 1 THESSALONIANS 2

SOUL-TO-SOUL MINISTRY

"We were ready to share with you not only the gospel of God but also our own selves." 1 THESSALONIANS 2:8

I've heard good men recommend a "professional distance" between the pastor and the church. I remember the counsel one experienced pastor offered: "You need to be friendly, but not friends. Don't joke, hang out, or fraternize." But here's the thing: Paul's relationships with those under his influence were neither *professional* nor *distant*. He had a mind-boggling breadth of relationships, all of which had a soul-stirring depth. His connection to people is especially evident in 1 Thessalonians 2.

This chapter reminds me a great deal of Paul's "leadership seminar" with the Ephesian elders in Acts 20:17–38. In both he speaks of the importance of personal integrity (Acts 20:18–19, 28–29; 1 Thessalonians 2:2–6, 9–10). In both he speaks of the courageous communication of Biblical truth (Acts 20:20–21, 24–27, 31–32, 35; 1 Thessalonians 2:2, 4, 13). And in both, he speaks of pastoral intimacy, evident in tears, in time with the flock, and in words of affection. Space requires that we focus on the last of these for now.

Disciple-makers should be gentle, like a nursing mother (v. 7). Apparently Paul's critics had accused him and his colaborers of coming to Thessalonica with ulterior motives. Reading the account of Paul's initial ministry in Thessalonica in Acts 17:1–9 shows what these accusations may have looked like. The fact that "not a few of the leading women" came to Christ through the ministry of Paul and Silas may have led to charges of greed or lust (Acts 17:4). In our text Paul reminds his readers that rather than gaining from them, Paul and Silas gave. He selects the perfect image of selfless devotion: a nursing mother. A mother cares for a helpless infant with unrivaled gentleness and persistence. And she does so unselfishly, knowing that the baby can give nothing in return. Her only motivation is love. What a tender example for disciple-makers to follow!

Disciple-makers should be encouraging, like a father with his children (vv. 11–12). I've often noted, both from Scripture and experience, how similar the roles of the pastor and the parent are. Paul has used a mother as an example of spiritual leadership; now he uses a father. Again, the illustration conveys intimacy and affection. But he especially highlights the *instruction* that good fathers provide for their children: "We exhorted . . . and encouraged . . . and charged" (v. 12). *Exhortation* describes a loving but firm challenge, or even warning. *Encouragement* tempers that exhortation with positive support. A *charge* is a solemn command from a respected leader, here focused on the need for the believers to "walk in a manner worthy of God," especially in light of their future participation in "his own kingdom and glory" (v. 12). Disciple-makers are to instruct and encourage like loving fathers, not harsh drill sergeants or cold executives.

Disciple-makers should share their souls as they share the truth (v. 8). Between the two tender examples of a nursing mother and a teaching father, Paul gives us what I think is the genius of Christian discipleship. Motivated by deep affection, Paul and Silas shared with the Thessalonians not only the truth but themselves ("our own souls," KJV). Ministry isn't just the conveying of information, like computer programming. It's intimate. It's personal. It's one life touching another. To disciple someone is to share your own soul with them.

The downside of the intimate relationships Paul describes is that they demand vulnerability. When pastors care this much, they get hurt, more deeply than people realize. It's tempting to close up to avoid such pain in the future. "Never again!" But opting for professional distance doesn't only prevent pain—it prevents influence. God has called us to invest our souls into those under our care. Like a mom, or a dad, or even an organ donor. And it's worth it!

Let the gospel make you an affectionate, gentle, and life-sharing disciple-maker.—CHRIS

DAY 12 — READ REVELATION 2:1–7

A CHURCH'S FIRST LOVE

"You have abandoned the love you had at first." REVELATION 2:4

God designed marriage, first and foremost, for companionship. Husband and wife should be best friends. Yet, at this most basic level, many faithful marriages suffer. As Michael Haykin summed it up, "It is all too common for spouses to live much of their lives together in separate worlds" (*The Christian Lover*, p. 73). That's a dangerous condition for a marriage! Similarly, that's a dangerous position for a church! God designed the marriage relationship to provide an instructive picture for the church. Just like God primarily designed marriage for loving companionship, he primarily designed salvation for a loving relationship with himself.

The book of Revelation, written around A.D. 95, opens with the ascended Lord Jesus Christ speaking his final instructions for his churches. He first speaks to the church in Ephesus, the same church that Paul spent three years planting (Acts 19), the same church that Timothy shepherded (1 Timothy 1:3), and the same church that had received Paul's letter from prison (Ephesians). When Jesus, through John, spoke to this same congregation (Revelation 2:1–7), the church at Ephesus was approaching its fiftieth anniversary.

Jesus commended the church at Ephesus for her faithfulness and doctrinal purity, but then rebuked her for coldness—for leaving her first love. In saying, "You have abandoned the love you had at first," Jesus alluded to words that the Lord had spoken to the unfaithful city of Jerusalem: "Remember the devotion of your youth, your love as a bride" (Jeremiah 2:2). Jesus' words to the church evoke thoughts of a newlywed couple who are head-over-heels in love with each other. This bride, the church at Ephesus, once had a deep love for Jesus himself but apparently let it grow cold throughout many years of faithful service. Did you know it's possible to be faithful but cold—to *faithfully serve* Jesus *without loving* Jesus? Did you know that it's possible to love good doctrine and to hate false doctrine, yet not love Jesus? It's not only possible; it's pervasive. In his excellent little book for pastors, *Liberating Ministry from the Success Syndrome*, Kent Hughes wrote:

> There is no success [in ministry] apart from loving God. . . . What appears at first glance to be success, is not necessarily success in God's economy. . . . It is possible to pastor a huge church and not love God. It is possible to design and preside over perfectly conceived and executed worship services and not love God. It is possible to preach insightful, biblical, Christ-exalting sermons and not love God. It is even possible to write books that deepen others' love for God and not love God. The truth is, it is more than just possible. For to our great sorrow, it is happening all too often (pp. 58–59).

Jesus counseled the cold Ephesian church to *remember* specific times in her past when her relationship with him was warmer; to *repent*—that is, to openly acknowledge her apathy and decidedly turn from it; and to *repeat* the kind of habits that characterized their relationship when it was at its closest. Failure to repent would lead the church, regardless of her doctrinal orthodoxy, to lose her testimony in her community and her identity as Jesus' church!

In view of such sobering threats, do you need to repent? Have you abandoned the love you had at first? It's so easy for Christians to experience this seemingly imperceptible shift. Early on we stand in worshipful wonder over the "kind of love the Father has given to us, that we should be called children of God" (1 John 3:1), but over time we develop an arrogant mindset that God is blessed to have us as his servants, and he somehow owes us more in life. Early on we humbly confess our desire to be near the Lord: "I would rather be a doorkeeper in the house of my God" (Psalm 84:10). Yet such love slowly hardens into bitterness over all the ministry burdens that we've carried for too long. Throughout the process, we lie to ourselves, believing that service for Christ somehow compensates for coldness in our relationship with him. Child of God, Jesus didn't save you so that he could squeeze decades of service out of you. He set his love on you because he wanted to experience your love for him in return. He saved you so you would live like you were created to live: loving God with all your heart. Jesus' isn't interested first in your labor, but in your love.

Let the gospel's goal—a relationship with God in Christ—be your first priority in life.—JOE

DAY 13 — READ 1 CORINTHIANS 2

GOSPEL SIMPLICITY

"So that your faith might not rest in the wisdom of men but in the power of God." 1 CORINTHIANS 2:5

We have a tendency to complicate ministry. Not that we aim to do that, but we live in a consumer culture driven by a mindset that thinks to be successful the church and the gospel need to be branded and marketed. We are not the first ones to think like this. The Corinthians were the original market-driven ministry proponents. Paul explains in 1 Corinthians 2:1–5 that his ministry at Corinth—which God used to establish that congregation—was just the opposite of what some of them were now promoting. Verse 5 reveals the purpose for his counter-cultural approach.

Paul's counter-cultural approach should shape our message. The verse ends with the words "in the power of God." To understand what Paul means, we must look back to 1 Corinthians 1:18: "For the word of the cross is folly to those who are perishing, but to us who are being saved it is the power of God." In context then, Paul is referring to the gospel message of Christ crucified. This is confirmed by v. 2: "For I decided to know nothing among you except Jesus Christ and him crucified." The Corinthians wanted him to adjust his message to make it more attractive to a target audience of sophisticated Greeks and skeptical Jews, but Paul refused. The wisdom and power of God are displayed in the message of the cross.

Paul's counter-cultural approach should shape our methods. The words "not rest on the wisdom of men" remind us that Paul would not shift away from the simple method of preaching the gospel plainly. The Greeks were famous for their rhetoric, and those who were skilled in it drew crowds. In our day of slick advertising and marketing mania, God's people have too often surrendered to these methods. We are told that we have to win people to ourselves before we can win them to Christ. We are told that we need to build our ministries around the felt needs of our target audience. The net result often is that the church is more like a shopping mall for consumers of spiritual goods and services than a place where "Christ and him crucified" is proclaimed as the answer for our true needs. Paul knew not only that the gospel was offensive to unbelievers but also that if you remove the offense of the gospel you lose the gospel's power. Only the Biblical method is the truly effective method.

Paul's counter-cultural approach should shape our mission. The words "your faith might not rest in the wisdom of men but in the power of God" summarize the reason why Paul preached what he did in the way he did. Those words sum up his mission: their salvation by faith in the gospel of Jesus Christ, accomplished by God's power, not his own. His rigid devotion to the Biblical message and method was grounded in his commitment to bring people to Christ. Because he rejected man-centered methods, when unbelievers came to faith in Christ it could only be explained by God's power, not by the communicator's shrewdness or skill. As he says in Romans 1:5, "Through [Christ] we have received grace and apostleship to bring about the obedience of faith for the sake of his name among all the nations." "For the sake of [God's] name" Paul sought to bring unbelievers to "the obedience of faith." People trusting Christ brings glory to God, so we should be zealous about seeing them come to faith in him.

Let the gospel control your ministry mindset so that your message, methods, and mission all flow from the cross of Christ toward the glory of God. —DAVE

DAY 14 — READ 2 JOHN & 3 JOHN

SEPARATION, COOPERATION, AND SCHISM

"We ought to support people like these." 3 JOHN 8

Christian separation is essential. And sometimes sinful. The same can be said of Christian cooperation. It's both a blessing and a curse. Churches have to determine when they should cooperate with other believers, when they might, and when they mustn't. It's complicated. Thankfully, we're not left to our own devices. Scripture deals with separation, cooperation, and schism in the "postcard" letters of 2 and 3 John.

We must separate from those who pervert the gospel. Second John teaches us that separation *protects* the gospel. In this short letter John commands Christian churches to defend the gospel from those who twist or deny it. It's true that John speaks often of love—in his Gospel, in 1 John, and even in 2 John (vv. 5–6). But he could also take the gloves off and fight when necessary. He warns against those who deny what Scripture teaches about the person and work of Christ (2 John 7–11). His estimate of a false teacher is unambiguous: "Such a one is the deceiver and the antichrist" (v. 8). He doesn't content himself with this warning, but he commands the church not to partner with false teachers in any way. Even hosting false teachers (v. 10)—much less partnering with them!—makes us partakers of their wickedness (v. 11). We must oppose error, not aid and abet it. Here 2 John joins a chorus of New Testament books in urging the church to defend the faith. Every New Testament book but Philemon (which accompanied Colossians) warns against false teachers.

We should cooperate with those who promote the gospel. Third John teaches us the flipside of what we learned from 2 John—that collaboration *promotes* the gospel. If we support false teachers, we are guilty by association (2 John). But if we support gospel teachers, we are partners by association: "fellow workers for the truth" (v. 8). Yes, there are enemies of the gospel. But there are also brothers who, though "strangers," are worthy of our support and partnership (vv. 5–6). John commends the church for showing hospitality to gospel workers, even those who were previously unknown to them. He calls for liberality both in extending friendship to others who love the gospel and in extending assistance to their gospel-rooted work.

We should beware of those who confuse those two categories. Third John also teaches us that schism *perverts* the gospel. Here's a quick synopsis of a conflict in the church addressed in 3 John. Gaius (v. 1) was a leader in the church who had been hospitable to those who preach the true gospel (vv. 3–8). As Mark Dever describes it, Gaius showed what it means to "*take* trouble for the gospel." But he and faithful Demetrius (v. 12) were opposed in the church by Diotrophes. Dever cites Diotrophes as an example of what it means to "*make* trouble for the gospel" (vv. 9–10). Diotrophes refused to fellowship with the Apostle John (v. 9). Worse yet, he refused to fellowship with anyone who *did* fellowship with the Apostle John (v. 10). He probably boasted that he was practicing what has been called first and second-degree separation. But because he was separating where he should have been collaborating—where there was gospel truth instead of the type of heresy mentioned in 2 John—he was actually practicing first and second-degree *schism*. Paul describes his words and actions as "wicked nonsense" (v. 10). And his motivation is telling: "He likes to put himself first," to be "preeminent" (v. 9, KJV). He was protecting turf, not truth. And thus he was a villain to be shunned, not imitated (v. 11).

The church must separate from those who promote error. The church must cooperate with those who promote truth. And the church must be very careful to know the difference between the two, lest we be guilty of the error of Diotrophes.

Let the gospel be so precious to you that you both protect *it and* promote *it.*—CHRIS

DAY 15 — READ ROMANS 12

GIFTS FOR HIS GLORY

"As each has received a gift, use it to serve one another, as good stewards of God's varied grace: whoever speaks, as one who speaks oracles of God; whoever serves, as one who serves by the strength that God supplies— in order that in everything God may be glorified through Jesus Christ. To him belong glory and dominion forever and ever. Amen." 1 PETER 4:10-11

The church is the body of Jesus Christ, designed and prepared to accomplish his mission here on earth. All believers are not only born of the Spirit but also given gifts for service on behalf of Jesus Christ. Gift-based ministry is a critical component of healthy church life. Other passages contribute to our understanding of gift-based ministry in the church, but the text above opens the door to at least four tremendous benefits.

Gift-based ministry changes the emphasis from programs to people. "Serve one another." The New Testament model for ministry is not the well-packaged, store-bought approach so common in our day. The church was not controlled by neat organizational structures, precisely defined time slots, and carefully crafted curricula. New Testament ministry was simple (vs. complex): Spirit-born and Spirit-gifted people ministering to each other.

Gift-based ministry distributes the work of ministry among the members of the church body. "As each has received a gift, use it." All believers have been equipped by God for service (see 1 Corinthians 12:7, 11; Romans 12:6). Ministry is not reserved for the professionals! The Head of the church has given gifts to each member of his body. Those gifts are graciously given as a stewardship responsibility, so every believer should desire to be a good steward of that grace. We must not receive that grace in vain! The unbiblical pattern of limiting ministry to a few specialists actually encourages believers to be poor stewards of God's grace.

Gift-based ministry enables the work to be infused with divine power since it is based on divine resources. "Whoever serves [should serve] . . . by the strength that God supplies." Ministry that flows out of the Spirit's work in a believer's life will be energized and effective through the Spirit's power. A spiritual gift is not like a magic charm that works just because we possess it. They can be neglected (1 Timothy 4:14) and may need to be stirred up (2 Timothy 1:6). We must also exercise them with clear, deliberate dependence on God so his strength can work through us.

Gift-based ministry makes the church more responsive to the work of Jesus Christ to glorify his Father. "Use [your gift] to serve one another . . . in order that in everything God may be glorified through Jesus Christ." Notice that even though it is the believers who are exercising their gifts, Peter says it is Jesus Christ who is glorifying his Father. That's because Jesus is working through gifted believers to accomplish the work. He gave the gifts. He empowers the gifts. If ministries are started, sustained, and staffed by believers who are consciously and carefully serving in the way Christ gifted them to serve, then we can have greater confidence that the church is doing God's will. Churches too often run ahead of the Lord with their own plans, resulting in a continual struggle to find workers to keep their programs running. If, however, the Lord wants something done in the church, he will supply the workers that are needed. After all, he knows more about and is more concerned with the Father's glory than we are!

Let the gospel gift of the Spirit's work your life control your ministry within the congregation so that God is glorified through Jesus Christ! —DAVE

DAY 16 — READ LUKE 15

A CHURCH OF PRODIGALS

"Now his older son was in the field, and as he came and drew near to the house, he heard music and dancing."
LUKE 15:25

All of us can relate to the joy of finding something that was lost—a lost set of keys, a lost phone, a lost purse, even a lost sock. Few things in life are more nagging than items you can't find. The main point of Luke 15 is repeated four times (vv. 6, 9, 23, 32): It's proper to celebrate when something lost gets found. In such cases celebration is not only allowable, but appropriate. Jesus, of course, is teaching the Pharisees that God not only tolerates lost sinners who repent but *celebrates* over them. In the parable that's often called "The Prodigal Son," there are two sons, and each represents a different kind of lostness.

If you're a rebel like the younger brother, repent and God will rejoice over you. Every person alive should be able relate to the younger brother. Like him we take all the resources that God has given us—our life, time, mind, money, sexuality, and abilities—and we instinctively say, "Thanks, God, but I'll do whatever I want with what you've given me. I don't really care about you. Just give me what I need to be happy apart from you." Naturally we're all like the lost son. We think the point of life is to have fun, when, in fact, the point of life is to have a good relationship with the Father. And, like the prodigal, we experience the emptiness of using God.

If you're a prodigal who's never "come home," you need to *repent* (vv. 7, 10). Repentance is a total change of heart. It's vividly described in the parable when the wayward son "came to himself," admitted his misery, fully accepted his own responsibility, and humbly asked his father to take him back even if only as a servant (vv. 17–19). What a powerful depiction of repentance! Have you ever decisively repented like that? I'm not talking about being sorry for an occasional screw up here and there. I'm talking about grieving over the natural bent of your life. If you never have, repent now. When a sinner repents, God is no grudging forgiver. He celebrates over you! Jesus knew that "there is joy before the angels of God over one sinner who repents" (vv. 7, 10, 22–27) because he knew what heaven was like. He had come from heaven. No doubt, Jesus had led such celebrations prior to his incarnation. He had vivid memories of dancing in heavenly parties over the repentance of lost individuals he would soon give his life to save.

If you're self-righteous like the older brother, realize you're as bad as your "little brother." The story of the two lost sons goes further than the two previous parables in Luke 15, the parables of the lost sheep and coin. It shows that there are two kinds of lost people—those who are rebellious and those who are religious. Rebellious lostness is more obvious. It looks like spending money on prostitutes and buying friends. When we see someone act like that, we all agree: "They're lost! What a reckless life!" Religious lostness is actually worse because those in that condition (as well as most around them) don't realize it. The older brother revealed just how lost he was by his calloused indifference to his brother, by his slavish obedience to his father's will, and by his selfish manipulation of his father's stuff. But, in the end, the rule-keeper had the same heart as the rule-breaker: His deep desire was to live his life apart from his father. That's legalism—religion without relationship—serving God, not for himself, but for what you can get out of him. It's ironic that when the younger brother returned home, he said, "If I could just be a *slave*, I'd be thrilled;" but the older brother thinks of his life in the father's house as *slavery* (vv. 19, 29).

The older brother in the parable describes most professing Christians on earth today. They believe that they're good people—better than most—who don't need to repent except for a mess up every now and then. Most professing Christians in the world need to be convinced that they *are* the down and outers—that they're not the upstanding people they imagine themselves to be. The only way that your church will reflect the Father's heart is if you first realize that you're a bunch of prodigals—a church full of people who were lost, joyously welcomed home by your gracious God, and now honored to serve him with your lives.

Let God's joyous heart in forgiveness lead you to frequently celebrate his grace.—JOE

DAY 17 — READ MATTHEW 5:23–25 & 18:15–17

KEEPING THE PEACE

"First be reconciled to your brother." MATTHEW 5:24

I read somewhere that seventy-eight percent of statistics are made up on the spot. I like that. Well, I have no hard numbers to verify my assertion, but I believe that most church problems are *personal* rather than *doctrinal* in nature. Sure, there are churches that deny sound doctrine, and their members should either bail or stage a prayerful mutiny rather than polish the brass on a sinking ship. But many churches that conscientiously preach the Word are sunk by broken relationships.

The Bible puts a premium on church unity. Jesus prayed for it (John 17:20–21). He taught that our mutual love would be a sign to the world that we are his disciples (John 13:35). The psalmist waxes eloquent about the beauty of unity (Psalm 133). And the Apostle Paul commands us to maintain Spirit-produced unity with the bond of peace (Ephesians 4:3). We don't have to *make* the unity; just don't *break* it. Two texts in Matthew show just how vital church peace is and how aggressively it must be protected and, when necessary, reclaimed.

Jesus commands the **criminal** *to seek reconciliation with his brother (Matthew 5:23–24).* As part of his Sermon on the Mount, Jesus teaches that reconciliation with an estranged brother is important—more important than even worship! Picture this: You are preparing to offer a sacrifice (in our day the equivalent might be a prayer, an act of service, or a financial offering). Prior to the act, your conscience reminds you that you've sinned against a brother. That's important. It's *your* fault: "Your brother has something against you" (v. 23). The specific offense is helpfully omitted, so you're expected to apply the general principle to your own situation, whatever it may be. Jesus commands you to seek reconciliation, urgently. In fact, you should set your gift aside, be reconciled to your brother, then return to your act of worship. Why? Because your fractured relationship with your Christian brother renders your worship unacceptable (much like 1 Peter 3:7). When you know you've sinned against a brother or sister in Christ, stop what you're doing. "Do not pass go." Seek reconciliation immediately by confessing your offense to him, asking for his forgiveness (without caveats or excuses), and restoring fellowship.

Jesus commands the **victim** *to seek reconciliation with his brother (Matthew 18:15–17).* Matthew 5 resonates with your sense of justice. The troublemaker should make the first move to correct the problem. But Matthew 18 obliterates that reasoning. "If your brother sins against you"—even if you're the *victim*!—you are still commanded to initiate reconciliation: "Go and tell him his fault, between you and him alone" with the hope that you might "gain your brother" (v. 15). Jesus leaves you no wiggle room. He doesn't tell you to harbor a well-deserved grudge. He doesn't allow you to avoid your brother. He certainly doesn't permit you to air the grievance to others—not even as a pseudo-sanctified "prayer request!" He tells you to go to him. Talk to him about his fault. Just between you and him. *Alone.* How well Jesus knows us! The hope—indeed, the prayer—is that you might gain a brother. You're not going to vent, or set the record straight, or get a pound of flesh. You're after something far more valuable: your *brother*.

Many offenses can be covered with love (1 Peter 4:8). But when there is a broken relationship and you are at fault, it is *your* job to go seek reconciliation. And if you've been sinned against, it's *your* job to go seek reconciliation. See? Anytime there is a breach of Christian fellowship, the onus is on *you* to help mend it. Don't wait for the other to move. You obey. Hopefully you'll meet each other on the road between your homes. But even if that's not the case, church unity is too vital to let offenses simmer. Our Savior says so!

Let the gospel that first joined you to your Christian brother mend your broken relationship.—CHRIS

DAY 18 — READ HEBREWS 13

COPING WITH PASTORAL TRANSITIONS

"Remember your leaders, those who spoke to you the word of God. Consider the outcome of their way of life, and imitate their faith. Jesus Christ is the same yesterday and today and forever." HEBREWS 13:7–8

Pastoral transitions are usually difficult times for churches. With the inimitable proclamation that "Jesus Christ is the same yesterday and today and forever," the writer to the weary Hebrew Christians points the way forward. Our stability as Christians doesn't rest primarily in our leaders but in Jesus, the same one in whom our leaders rested. Leaders come and go, but Jesus remains the same. If we've had a leader who has exemplified strong, persevering trust in the Lord Jesus, we should respect him, meditate on his life, and imitate him. However, we must not cling to him as if our stability rests in him. No, what makes a great leader great is how he, for his relatively brief ministry, pointed to the unchanging Christ whose glory is unveiled in the letter to the Hebrews.

Great church leaders trust Jesus, God's Son. The first chapter of Hebrews proclaims Jesus as the unique Son of God. God's angels are just servants, but the uncreated Son is enthroned with God and receives the same worship as God the Father. Great leaders are mere servants who love to gaze on the Son and proclaim the wonders of his majesty and love. Great church leaders regularly say, "Don't look to me, look to Christ." Church leaders are not the objects of our faith but examples of faith whom we should imitate.

Great church leaders rest in Jesus, the sympathetic High Priest. God's glorious Son took on flesh and became our brother (2:17). As our brother, Jesus became our sympathetic Mediator—our great High Priest who is uniquely able to understand our weaknesses because he experienced the same kinds of temptations as we do, "yet without sin" (4:15–16). Jesus Christ sympathizes with us in all our struggles. Exemplary leaders constantly admit their weaknesses. They pray desperately and boldly, and through Christ they "find grace to help in time of need." When they transition, the merciful and faithful High Priest remains the same.

Great church leaders proclaim Jesus, the once-for-all Sacrifice. In Hebrews 5–10 the author's main point is that Jesus is a *better priest than the Levites* who offered a *better sacrifice than lambs* and mediated a *better covenant than the Law*. Jesus' one-time sacrifice of himself on the cross was the only sacrifice that has ever actually cleansed sinners and assuaged God's holy wrath (Hebrews 10:1-18). Great leaders proclaim the holy glories of Jesus' substitutionary atonement. That theme is no less glorious after they depart.

Great church leaders look to Jesus, the Sustainer. The eleventh chapter of Hebrews is filled with heroes who persevered by faith—heroes like Noah, Abraham, Moses, and Rahab. All of these heroes fixed their eyes on the promises of God and endured by faith. According to Hebrews 12:2, Jesus Christ is both the example for and object of our faith. Exemplary believers endure trials *like Christ, by looking to Christ*. They endure seasons of tragedy, accusation, conflict, departures, disappointments, exhaustion, depression, and sickness by "looking to Jesus." You will find stability not by keeping your eyes fixed on your church leaders but by keeping your eyes fixed on Christ.

Great church leaders point to Jesus, the great Shepherd. Jesus Christ, the risen Lamb, is "the great shepherd of the sheep" (Hebrews 13:20). Members of gospel-preaching churches must regularly remind themselves that their current leaders are only "undershepherds." Jesus is the church's "great pastor."

Jesus is the unchanging Son, Sympathizer, Sacrifice, Sustainer, and Shepherd. He's the only one that Christians *need* for stability. Great church leaders trust Jesus and proclaim his glories to the churches that they're responsible to lead. They recognize that their ministries are quickly fading, and they help the believers under their care find stability in the only one who is "the same yesterday and today and forever."

Let the glory of Christ stabilize you in seasons of pastoral transition.—JOE

DAY 19 — READ EPHESIANS 2

THE CHURCH AS A MULTI-ETHNIC TAPESTRY

"There is neither Jew nor Greek . . . for you are all one in Christ." GALATIANS 3:28

The President of the United States has noted that "the most segregated hour of American life occurs on Sunday morning." It's true. People of various ethnicities (a word that is much better than *races* as there is but one human race) work together, cheer for sports teams together, and go to school together. But with rare exceptions, we don't worship together. I think that's a travesty. I could argue that the church is *behind* the world when it comes to diversity—yet we have the very thing that makes deep-rooted unity possible. Since my arrival in Gwinnett County (northeast of Atlanta, and one of the most diverse counties in America), I've prayed and preached that Killian Hill Baptist Church should be as diverse as our area. If we *reach* our community, we'll *reflect* our community. By God's grace, it's happening, and God gets the glory because it was his idea. Long before there was a Civil Rights Movement, or Political Correctness, or Affirmative Action, our Lord gave us a blueprint for unified diversity in Ephesians 2:11-16.

Paul wrote to the Ephesians that "before Christ" they were dead and damned. Ephesians 2:1–10 describe the grace that brings dead sinners to life and makes them into a living "tapestry" or "work of art" that displays Jesus' glory (v. 10). But the passage doesn't stop at verse 10, though we usually do in our studies of the text. It goes on in the next six verses to describe the various *colors* of that tapestry. Specifically, the Bible tells us that the gospel unites people of different cultures and ethnicities (here, Jews and Gentiles) into one new creation: the church!

The gospel unites sinners with God. Before Christ, all sinners were estranged from God. Non-Jews were especially distant from God. William Hendriksen describes their plight (based on Ephesians 2:11-13) as "Christless, stateless, friendless, hopeless, and Godless" (*New Testament Commentary: Ephesians,* p. 129). "But God" (vv. 4, 13). God intervened, through Jesus, and made a way for sinners to be reconciled to God. The removal of the sin that separated us from God is beautifully portrayed in Matthew 27:51 by the tearing of the temple veil which itself symbolized the estrangement that commenced at the Fall (Genesis 3:31). The veil was torn, and sinners can have fellowship with God (see *Gospel Meditations for Prayer*, Day 26). But there's more!

The gospel also unites sinners with each other. Jesus didn't only tear the veil between us and God. He also "made us both [Jews and Gentiles] one and has broken down in his flesh the dividing wall of hostility" (v. 14). Paul alludes here to an actual wall that was prominent in Herod's temple, restricting non-Jews to the Court of the Gentiles at the threat of death! Acts 22:21-24 records a riot that ensued when Jews erroneously thought Paul had brought a Gentile into the Jewish section of the Temple.

Jesus undid that nonsense. He *is*, has *made*, and has *preached* "peace" (vv. 14, 15, 17). When we are born again, we are united both to Christ and to Christians—even Christians of different cultures. The church is "one new man" in which breaches are bridged (v. 15; Galatians 3:27-29). As my friend JD Crowley has powerfully stated, "The cross is a dagger in the heart of racism." Amen! Prejudice is anti-gospel. Segregation is anti-gospel. We mustn't expect it or accept it as "the way it is." It's "the way it was," pre-Jesus. Now he both prescribes and provides peace through his glorious gospel.

Hear John Piper's good words on the bridge-building power of the gospel:

> Religious tradition and human opinion are powerless to create and sustain a life of Christ-exalting ethnic diversity and harmony. Only a deeply rooted grasp of what God has achieved through the gospel of Jesus can do this (*Bloodlines*, p. 211).

Let the gospel make you passionate about ethnic unity, even in your local church. —CHRIS

DAY 20 — READ JAMES 5:13-18

PRAY LIKE YOU MEAN IT

"The prayer of a righteous person has great power as it is working." JAMES 5:16

Do you pray like it really matters? Seriously, when you pray, do you approach it as if the outcome of your praying depends at all on your praying? I don't mean these to be merely rhetorical questions aimed at stirring your thought. I mean for each person who reads these words to truly ask and answer that question—Do you pray like it really matters that you pray?

This question may be tougher than it looks because it forces us to wrestle with the difficult subject of divine sovereignty and human responsibility. Without, I hope, oversimplifying things, it seems to me that there are three different ways you can try to harmonize divine sovereignty and human responsibility. And your practice of prayer will be directly affected by your understanding of this apparent tension.

The first viewpoint: "God is unmoved by my prayers." On one hand there is a view of sovereignty that comes close to saying that God will do what he is going to do whether we pray or not. The logic seems to be that God's sovereignty would be compromised if he "needs" man to pray in order to accomplish his will. But this view is flawed by injecting the word "needs" into the equation. There is a huge gap between saying that God will accomplish his purposes regardless of our prayers (or lack thereof) and that God is dependent on our prayers. It seems impossible to hold the views "regardless of our prayers" and "our prayer really matters" at the same time.

The second viewpoint: "God is powerless apart from my prayers." At the other end of the spectrum is the view that God really can't do some things until people ask him. This view, in an attempt to preserve human responsibility, establishes a system in which God is limited by man's will. God would do certain things if he could, but without the prayers of his people is not able to do what he wants. While this view makes a strong case that your prayers really matter, it sadly leaves you praying to a God different from the one revealed in Scripture—the one who is able to do whatever he pleases (Psalm 115:3) and to act even when his people don't pray as they should (Isaiah 59:15-16).

The third viewpoint: "God chooses to work through my prayers." Between these two views is one that seeks to honor both truths taught in Scripture—that God is sovereign and man is responsible. These truths are compatible, not contradictory. We probably never will be able to comprehend completely the intricate relations between them, but we are bound by Scripture to honor them. God is not dependent on me, but his independence does not mean that he does not relate to and interact with me. His plan includes the believer's participation—God ordains *the means* as well as *the ends*, and this is where prayer gains its significance. God has chosen to accomplish his purposes through the prayers of his people; therefore, his people are responsible to pray so that those purposes will be accomplished.

What does it look like when we pray like we really mean it? Elijah, in the passage above, serves as good example for us. Rather than vainly repeating a bunch of cliches, he fervently and specifically presented his request ("he prayed fervently that it might not rain"), a request based on God's promises and warnings to Israel (see Deuteronomy 28:23–24). Serious prayer is always specific and Scriptural. If we take God and his Word seriously, then we'll pray like it really matters.

Let the gospel privilege of prayer sink deeply into your heart so that you believe the promises of God and pray like you really do!—DAVE

DAY 21 — READ EPHESIANS 4:1–16

THE EXPENDABLE PASTOR

"To equip the saints for the work of the ministry." EPHESIANS 4:12

It is remarkable how a few seconds can alter an entire life. I had an experience like that as I was wrapping up my seminary training. I had read thousands of pages during my preparation for ministry, but a few sentences from Augustus Strong's *Systematic Theology* just leapt off the page:

> That minister is most successful who gets the whole body to move, and who renders the church independent of himself. The test of his work is not while he is with them, but after he leaves them. Then it can be seen whether he has taught them to follow him, or to follow Christ; whether he has led them to the formation of habits of independent Christian activity, or whether he has made them passively dependent upon himself (p. 908).

Strong's words resonated with me because I knew they were an expression of Biblical truth. Paul exemplified this kind of expendability in his ministry. He urged Timothy to entrust what he had learned to faithful men who could in turn teach others (2 Timothy 2:2). His job description of the pastor-teacher in Ephesians 4:11–12 focuses on equipping the church for "every member ministry."

Pastors are God's gifts to the church (v. 11). The ascended Christ gave the church gifts through the indwelling Holy Spirit (vv. 7–10). Those gifts are cataloged in Romans 12, 1 Corinthians 12, and 1 Peter 4. But it is in Ephesians 4 that Paul speaks of what I call "office gifts." He lists four: "And he gave the apostles, the prophets, the evangelists, and the shepherds and teachers" (v. 11). I believe the first two were foundational (Ephesians 2:20) and therefore temporary. The last two (Greek grammar makes it clear that "shepherds and teachers" refer to only one office) describe those who found churches (evangelists) and those who continue with churches (pastors). Pastors are described as shepherds who *lead* the flock and teachers who *feed* the flock.

The pastor's job is to equip the entire church for ministry (v. 12). The pastor is "to equip the saints for the work of ministry, for building up the body of Christ." He intentionally equips the body, preparing and then unleashing the whole church to serve God and each other. The effective pastor isn't a hired gun. He isn't a demagogue. He isn't a one-man show. The effective pastor works hard to render himself expendable, training the body—especially faithful men (2 Timothy 2:2)—so that they don't need him. That's a different mindset than the "man of God" mentality that takes a top-down approach to ministry and frequently reminds the flock to "touch not God's anointed." But such an enabling, encouraging, self-effacing pastor insures that the church will grow to "mature manhood" (v. 13), will grow beyond spiritual childhood (v. 14), and will be "held together by every joint with which it is equipped, when each part is working properly" (v. 16). See that? The church is strongest, and safest, and most sustainable when "every joint" and "each part" is functioning as God intended. The pastor's job is to make sure that happens—by teaching, by equipping, and sometimes by getting out of the way.

I internalized Augustus Strong's words. But I didn't anticipate how powerfully they'd be put to the test in my own ministry. After fifteen years as the pastor of Tri-County Bible Church in Madison, Ohio—the last seven of those alongside Joe Tyrpak—I sensed the Lord calling me elsewhere. It broke my heart to leave people I so loved, many of whom I'd led to Christ. But the church was ready. I was expendable. Leaders were strong. I became Joe's assistant for a short time. And when I moved away, the church moved on, stronger than ever. Just as it should be.

Pastor, equip the whole body to do things you cannot, to take care of each other, and to outlive you. Church member, don't just show up and expect the pastor to do the work of ministry. Grow. Sharpen your skills. Use your gifts. And labor alongside the rest of the body for God's glory!

Let the gospel make you ultimately dependent on the only perfect Shepherd. —CHRIS

DAY 22 — READ EPHESIANS 4:17–5:21

LIVING UNDER THE INFLUENCE

"Do not get drunk with wine, for that is debauchery, but be filled with the Spirit." EPHESIANS 5:18

There's a frequent disconnect between Christian knowledge and Christian living. Whether a believer's struggle is with anger, bitterness, lust, or worry, I've had numerous conversations that include a common plea: "I know I'm failing, and I know what my life should look like, but how do I actually get there?"

Empowerment to live like Christ comes to us the same way it came to Christ. The Servant of the Lord accomplished his mission in the power of God's Spirit (Isaiah 42:1). If Jesus, God become man, fulfilled his calling by the empowerment of God's Spirit, then we who are much weaker most certainly need the same empowerment. The power to live the Christian life comes supernaturally. It's a power that must "come to rest upon you"—overtake you—intoxicate you. When Paul teaches the necessity of Spirit-controlled living in Ephesians 5, he says that drunkenness with alcohol leads to debauchery, but drunkenness with God's Spirit leads to Christlikeness. Living under the influence of alcohol leads individuals to lose control, while living under the influence of God's Spirit leads to believers to sobriety and self-control (Galatians 5:23). So, exactly how do you get *intoxicated* with the Spirit? If you compile all of Paul's references to the Spirit in his succinct letter to the church at Ephesus, I think you get a good idea of how to live under the Spirit's influence. Here are five ways.

You must be indwelt by the Spirit's presence. When individuals hear the gospel and personally believe in Jesus, they are "sealed with the promised Holy Spirit" (Ephesians 1:13). To be sealed is to be permanently marked as belonging to God. If you don't have God's Spirit, you don't belong to God (Romans 8:9). There's no chance you can be controlled by God's Spirit if you've never believed the gospel.

You must be armed with the Spirit's sword. In Ephesians 6:17 Paul calls the message of the Bible "the sword of the Spirit." Earlier in the letter Paul had taught that God revealed his will "to his holy apostles and prophets by the Spirit" (Ephesians 3:5). So if you're going to be intoxicated with the Spirit, you must arm yourself with an accurate knowledge of what the apostles and prophets wrote "by the Spirit."

You must gather at the Spirit's temple. Paul describes the church as the temple of the Holy Spirit (Ephesians 2:22). The presence of God is found in a gospel-preaching congregation—where two or three are gathered in Jesus' name. A church's auditorium is not "the sanctuary." The gathering of the church's members is! We get concentrated doses of the Spirit when we gather with other believers to pool our resources for the Great Commission, to observe the ordinances, to learn the apostles' doctrine, and to pray together (Acts 2:42). When you're struggling as a Christian, sometimes the hardest thing to do is to gather with the church. But, if power for the Christian life comes through the Spirit's intoxication, you need to go to the Spirit's temple.

You must pray in the Spirit's power. Three times Paul urges Christians to pray in the Spirit (Ephesians 2:18; 3:16; 6:18). To pray in the Spirit means to pray with the Spirit's full assurance of access to God the Father. If you regularly give yourself to praying boldly for the advance of the gospel and the good of the church, you'll "get drunk with" the Spirit.

You must be sensitive to the Spirit's grief. Paul exhorts believers, "Do not grieve the Holy Spirit of God" (Ephesians 4:30). The Holy Spirit of God is not some impersonal force but a person with emotional capacity. The Spirit who indwells me is grieved when I choose to sin, especially when I am unkind, cruel, and bitter toward other believers. By contrast, I live "under the influence" of the Spirit when I'm sensitive to his grief and repent of my sin.

The Spirit of God is the "how to" of the Christlike life. He empowered *the* Servant of the Lord, and he empowers servants of the Lord. In order to fulfill God's calling for your life, God's Spirit must intoxicate you.

Let the power that rested on God's Servant rest on you. —JOE

DAY 23 — READ 1 PETER 1:13-25

THE HOLY CHURCH

"You shall be holy, for I am holy." 1 PETER 1:16 & LEVITICUS 11:44

"We're not the good people. We're sinners in need of God's grace." I often remind myself and the people I pastor of these truths. The fact that we're in church on Sunday morning, on time(ish), and more or less "dressed up" doesn't change the fact that we're all rivals for the title "chief of sinners" (1 Timothy 1:15). We haven't arrived. We're under construction. A candid church slogan would read as follows: "Grace Bible Church: We're a Mess!"

But there's a danger to that kind of "Spiritual Self-Identity" (*Gospel Meditations for Men*, Day 3). While an awareness of our sinfulness is necessary, we must resist seeing sin as "normal" for the Christian. It's easy for those who recognize their deep sinfulness to almost rejoice in it. Every failure, every outburst, every lapse becomes little more than a reminder of our sound theology ("I'm so bad!") and a celebration of God's grace ("God's so good!"). In Paul's words, we "continue in sin that grace may abound" (Romans 6:1). Here's the thing: That's hubris, not humility. Paul's response is "May it never be," translated less accurately but more memorably in the KJV as "God forbid!"

The church is to be known in the world as a *holy* people. Yes, that's our standing in Christ, in spite of ourselves (1 Corinthians 1:1). But it's also our new *nature*—we're not just the same people clothed in imputed righteousness (as beautiful as the truth of justification is). We're new people, *regenerated* and therefore growing in daily, habitual righteousness (sometimes called *imparted righteousness*). We're not sinless—but we're sinning less. We're fleeing sin and pursuing righteousness. We're progressing. We're growing. We're changing. We're under construction. When we say, "Pardon our spiritual dust," we don't mean a sandbox of sin in which we play but the sawdust that shows that we're working to overcome sin. Christ's church should be a holy church!

First Peter 1:13-25 is a strong antidote to "continuing in sin." Peter argues for our holy conduct with several timeless truths:

We must be holy because we are God's children (v. 14). We are welcomed as God's children by his grace—and transformed into "obedient children" by that same grace.

We must be holy because we cannot continue in our "former ignorance" (v. 14). We live in a world of "before and after" pictures that highlight "extreme makeovers." Well, Scripture provides such a contrast, pointing out the extreme change that Christ makes in our daily lives, not just our eternal destinies.

We must be holy because God is holy (v. 15). Our union to the thrice-holy God demands that we be holy as well—again, not just in our position in Christ, but in "all [our] conduct."

We must be holy because God commands it (v. 16). Peter quotes Leviticus 11:44 and demonstrates that God's command that his people pursue holiness is as essential in this age of grace as it was under the Law.

We must be holy because Jesus shed his blood to make us so (vv. 18-19). Here is the *coup de grâce*. These precious verses tell us that Jesus shed his priceless blood not just to redeem us from hell but to ransom us from *sin*—"from the futile ways inherited from your forefathers." Jesus bled to make us holy, both in our standing and in our walking.

Consider this lament from Spurgeon:

> An unholy Church! It is useless to the world, and of no esteem among men. It is an abomination, hell's laughter, heaven's abhorrence. The worst evils which have ever come upon the world have been brought upon her by an unholy church (*Morning and Evening*, June 26).

Let the gospel inspire you and empower you to be holy in your everyday life.—CHRIS

DAY 24 — READ REVELATION 4–5

NEVER FORGET THE BLOOD

"You were slain, and by your blood you ransomed people for God." REVELATION 5:9

Sometimes Christians think of the death of Jesus as "milk, not meat." Confusing the elementary response to the gospel (i.e., repentance and faith) with the gospel message itself, Christians wrongly imagine that the message of the crucifixion is crucial only for unbelievers and baby Christians. They think it's something that mature Christians "move past," and they fail to recognize that Christian maturity involves a deeper understanding, appreciation, and application of the person and work of Jesus Christ. The heart of the gospel message is something that believers will never forget and must never forget. The book of Revelation refers five times to Jesus' blood, and in so doing reveals five reasons why believers will never forget the blood.

Jesus' blood freed you from sin's chains (Revelation 1:5). Jesus "freed [you] from [your] sins by his blood." Here every offense you've ever committed against God is pictured as a chain. Do you remember the chains that bound you? You were confined in chains of pride and ambition, chains of covetousness and lust, chains of bitterness and addiction. The mighty blood of Jesus broke ten thousand chains that were confining you! You were a helpless prisoner, and you'll forever praise Jesus for his chain-breaking blood.

Jesus' blood bought you out of sin's slavery (Revelation 5:9). Saints in heaven praise the risen Lamb: "You were slain, and by your blood you ransomed people for God." You were a slave in need of ransom, the price paid to free a slave. Do you remember your unpayable debts? You kept sinning, descending deeper into debt, and you had no ability to pay God back. Yet, when you were helpless, Jesus paid your debts with his blood. You'll forever praise him—along with others from every culture, class, ethnicity, and age—for his blood.

Jesus' blood cleansed you from sin's stains (Revelation 7:14). When you stand in God's presence you'll be dressed in white, symbolizing that your life is spotlessly clean. God does not allow one bit of filth into his presence. The bloody crucifixion of Jesus provided the only cleansing agent for sin's stains because only the crucifixion of Jesus completely satisfied the justice of God for our crimes. If you have believed the gospel, you are fit for the presence of a holy God, not because you weren't "all that bad," but because the robe of your life is blood-washed.

Jesus' blood ensures your victory over every Satanic attack (Revelation 12:11). As Jesus' follower, you are the constant target of Satanic accusations, doubts, and opposition. Yet, amidst the onslaught of these flaming arrows, you must never think that Satan is *winning*. He's not! Satan is dying. The serpent's skull was crushed at Golgotha, and he is flailing in the throes of defeat. Struggling Christian, take courage. Jesus has won. When you're asked in heaven, "How did you overcome?" for all eternity, you'll answer: "[I] conquered him by the blood of the Lamb."

Jesus' blood assures you of final justice (Revelation 19:13). The conquering King "is clothed in a robe dipped in blood." That's not the blood of his enemies, but the stains of his own blood. In his glorious second coming, Jesus' military uniform will still bear the marks of his gory first coming. His blood-dipped robe will remind you that you're a part of his army because he died for you. You're wearing white because he's wearing red. His blood-dipped robe, like military decoration, will also encourage you with his past record of victory. Since he already conquered sin and death, he'll win this final battle with ease. When Jesus returns in glory and you appear with him, you'll still be glorying in his blood.

For all eternity you'll glory in the blood of the Lamb. Don't allow yourself to get bored with it today. Don't think you need to move on to truths that are "more meaty." Jesus' crucifixion should be explicitly remembered every time his church gathers for worship. It's the foundation of your prayers, the basis of comfort in your trials, the substance of your songs, the essence of communion, and the heart of Biblical teaching. Never forget the blood.

Let the gospel be something you never "move past." —JOE

DAY 25 — READ 1 CORINTHIANS 10:32–11:1 & GALATIANS 1:6-10

PLEASING GOD OR PEOPLE?

"I try to please everyone in everything I do, not seeking my own advantage, but that of many, that they may be saved." 1 CORINTHIANS 10:33

The label "people-pleaser" is a dreaded one, isn't it? It immediately conjures up ideas of insecurity and instability. Yet, the text above actually encourages us to be a people-pleaser. And it is not the only text that does so. Look at Romans 15:2: "Let each of us please his neighbor for his good, to build him up." Twice Paul directs us toward pleasing others. But it gets a little tricky when we consider that Paul also tells us *not* to please others! Consider these verses:

> For am I now seeking the approval of man, or of God? Or am I trying to please man? If I were still trying to please man, I would not be a servant of Christ (Galatians 1:10).

> But just as we have been approved by God to be entrusted with the gospel, so we speak, not to please man, but to please God who tests our hearts (1 Thessalonians 2:4).

At first glance these verses seem to contradict each other. How can Paul say he is not trying to please men (Galatians 1:10, 1 Thessalonians 2:4) and that each of us is to please his neighbor (Romans 15:2) and that he personally tried to "please everyone in everything [he did]" (1 Corinthians 10:33)? Can you really be committed to both pleasing people and not pleasing people? Don't you have to choose one or the other?

Although some may be comfortable leaving Paul in a hopeless contradiction, those who believe the Bible is God's inspired Word know that this cannot be a genuine contradiction, but that it only *appears* to be a contradiction. So how do these two truths (pleasing God, pleasing people) relate to each other as complementary rather than contradictory?

The key is in the context of these verses. The "pleasing God, not men" texts are found in contexts where Paul is defending the content of his gospel and preaching. Since the message he had received was from God, he had no right to alter it or tamper with it in order to make it more acceptable and pleasing to people. To do that would be to disobey and displease God.

The "pleasing people" texts are in the context of reaching unbelievers (1 Corinthians 10:33) and ministering to believers (Romans 15:2). They focus on making adjustments in our actions and attitudes that may be hindering us from reaching and edifying people. Very near to both texts are statements that show that pleasing both unbelievers and believers is subordinate to pleasing God. First Corinthians 10:31 is clear that the choices made in application of verse 33 must be done for God's glory. Romans 15:7 is equally clear that the goal is that the relationships among believers would bring glory to God. Whatever Paul is saying about "pleasing people" cannot be cut off from its purpose— glorifying (therefore pleasing) God. Paul isn't suggesting that you can do *anything* to please people.

What seem to be contradictory ideas actually fit well together once we recognize their proper relationship to each other. Pleasing God is given first place, so rather than contradicting each other, "pleasing God" and "pleasing others" can fulfill each other. If God has first place, then we are positioned well to serve others (whether unbelievers or believers). In fact, we cannot truly serve them well if we don't have God in first place. The deepest, greatest need of all humans is a proper relationship to God, so the highest, greatest service we can do for all humans is to point them to God. Because God "desires all people to be saved and to come to the knowledge of the truth" (1 Timothy 2:4), he is pleased when we give the needs of others priority over our own in order to win them to Christ or build them up in the faith. We please God by pleasing others for the sake of the gospel.

Let the gospel protect you from sinful people-pleasing and transform you into someone who pleases others for their good and God's glory!—DAVE

DAY 26 — READ 1 THESSALONIANS 4:13–5:11

THE GOSPEL & CHURCH GRIEF

"Since we believe that Jesus died and rose again, even so, through Jesus, God will bring with him those who have fallen asleep." 1 THESSALONIANS 4:14

Any Christian who has grieved the loss of a believing friend or family member can attest that the grief is not something that ever really stops. It's just something that you learn to live with. In Paul's first letter to the church at Thessalonica, written two decades after the death and resurrection of Jesus, he describes the reality of grief when fellow believers die. As Mike Barrett puts it, "Not sorrowing as the world sorrows does not mean not sorrowing at all" (*God's Unfailing Purpose*, pp. 192–93). Trusting the Lord doesn't mean that you're forever smiling. A Christian's faith and a Christian's tears are not mutually exclusive. Grief is the right and appropriate response to death. It's okay to cry, even to be disturbed in your grief (see John 11:33, 35) because death is not part of God's original creation. Paul teaches not that Christian grief is inappropriate but that it is not hopeless. When Christians grieve, we're full of hope—hope in the glorious return of Jesus. Paul reveals three specific details about Jesus' coming that comfort believers who have said goodbye to Christian loved ones.

When Jesus returns, every Christian who has died will be raised. The resurrection of Christians is certain because of the resurrection of Christ (v. 14). Paul received special revelation from Jesus about the order in which Christians will meet the Lord. Those Christians who have "fallen asleep" will actually be raised before the Christians who are still alive are gathered (v. 15). As the language of sleep implies, the bodies of believers who have died are only temporarily inactive. They're going to live again. The death of their physical bodies will be as short-lived as a night of sleep. The bodies of these departed saints will awake to three loud noises that start Jesus' military advance—"a cry of command," "the voice of the archangel," and "the sound of the trumpet of God" (v. 16). What an alarm clock! The commander of God's army, Jesus himself, will issue the commanding shout that raises the dead (see John 5:25). Grieving believers, with one resounding noise, your believing loved ones will be raised, and your grief will come to an end.

When Jesus returns, every Christian who is alive will be raptured. If you are alive when Jesus descends, you are going to be "caught up together with" those who have just been raised from the dead, and you're going to "meet the Lord in the air" (v. 17). The words *caught up* and *meet* continue the military imagery, describing how believers will be carried off by force to encounter an approaching entourage (as in Matthew 25:6 and Acts 28:15). In other words, Paul is conveying a surprise rescue of POWs who have been awaiting their release. He implies that Christians are POWs, living in a world that's ruled by our enemy. We who are still alive have this great hope that Jesus is coming to rescue us. With his archangel, his army of angels, and his resurrected saints, Jesus is going to storm the kingdom of this world, and we who are still alive will be extracted by the world's rightful Ruler. Grieving believer, what's revealed here should fuel your hope and your holiness. It's just a matter of time until the Commander comes.

When Jesus returns, Christians will be reunited with each other and with Jesus. All those who have trusted Jesus will be reunited in fellowship with every other believer in Jesus. Even more, all who have trusted in Jesus will meet him face to face and will never again be separated from him. This grand reunion is what will make heaven heaven.

Do you believe the events described here will actually happen? Notice that it's all hinged on the historic events of the gospel (v. 14). The question you have to ask is not, "Will the return of Jesus actually happen?" but, "Did the resurrection of Jesus actually happen?" The one who died and rose again for us is the same one coming for us. The risen King will return. He's going to raid this province that's temporarily under enemy control. And, as he regathers his people, not one believer, dead or alive, will go missing.

Let the gospel encourage your grief to be mixed with solid hope. —JOE

DAY 27 — READ 2 CORINTHIANS 8–9

GRACE-INSPIRED GIVING

"Excel in this act of grace also." 2 CORINTHIANS 8:7

Giving is a tough topic. I've heard pastors criticized for talking about it *too little* and for talking about it *too much*. I confess that I'm rather bashful about asking people to give to support the ministry of the church. It's awkward. But as uncomfortable as the topic may be to us, the Bible speaks of money—and offerings—consistently and candidly. Giving comes up frequently in Scripture, and it should come up with equal frequency in churches that preach the whole counsel of God. "Offering" passages can be found throughout the Bible, but 2 Corinthians 8–9 encapsulates instructions on giving for New Testament believers.

First, consider what the text doesn't say. It's curious to me that the primary passage that details giving in the local church doesn't mention tithing (giving one-tenth of your income to the work of the Lord; the word *tithe* means *tenth*). It's just not there. That's not to say there's a problem with the *principle* of tithing. I don't think tithing is legalistic or outdated. Though some tie it to the Old Testament Law, the tithe was actually introduced in Genesis 14:19–20, *prior* to the Law. Many find that it's helpful to continue the tithe principle by giving ten percent of their earnings to Christ's church. I commend that practice. But with an eye on 2 Corinthians 8–9, I'd encourage you to think of ten percent as a starting line, not a finish line. This passage repeatedly speaks of giving as an act of *grace* (8:1, 6, 7, 9, 19; 9:8, 14, 15), and I'm confident that grace will motivate even more generosity than law. Let's consider what the text *does* say. Here's a quick overview of what grace-based giving looks like:

Give sacrificially (8:1–4). Paul cites the Macedonian Christians as examples of giving. They gave not because they were wealthy but despite their "severe test of affliction" and "extreme poverty" (v. 2). They gave "beyond their means" (v. 3), literally "begging" Paul to take their money (v. 4). Why? Read on.

Give spiritually (8:5). The Macedonians didn't give their money instead of their time or hearts, like some Christians today who assume that giving is an easy alternative to serving. No, they gave beyond their means specifically because they had given "themselves first to the Lord." When God has *us*, it's much easier for him to have what's *ours*, as well.

Give lovingly (8:8–9, 24; 9:15). Twice in these chapters Christ's crucifixion is given as the ultimate example of sacrifice (8:9; 9:15)—and the ultimate motivation for our sacrificial giving. The fact that "Jesus paid it all" should motivate us to give in response, as proof of our love (8:8, 24). We love because he loved. And we give because he gave.

Give intentionally (8:10–15; 9:1–5). Yes, giving is a grace. But it's also a skill in which we should excel (8:7). Paul urged the Corinthians to carry out their intentions. You have wanted to give. Great! Now plan for it. Budget for it. Cut spending for it. But do it.

Give joyfully (9:7). Most Christians know the phrase "God loves a cheerful giver." The point is not that we snicker as the offering plate is passed. But truly, it should *delight* us to give. We should decide on an amount in our hearts, then give with joy, not regret. Let me illustrate. I get no joy from paying my mortgage, my taxes, or my utility bills. But it is indeed a joy to write a check to my local church, thanking God for the privilege and praying he'll use it for his glory.

Give believingly (9:6–14). You don't give to get. That's a trick of the Prosperity Gospel, not the Scriptures. But the Bible does challenge us to give with the promise that God will provide for our needs. He can meet our needs better that we can. He can help us reap more than we so. He is more generous than we are. Give audaciously, and see what amazing things the Lord will do!

Let the gospel free you from materialism and make you a joyful giver to the Lord.—CHRIS

DAY 28 — READ 1 CORINTHIANS 5

THE MOST BASIC RESPONSIBILITY OF CHURCH MEMBERSHIP

"For what have I to do with judging outsiders? Is it not those inside the church whom you are to judge?"
1 CORINTHIANS 5:12

People often ask me, "Is 'church membership' Biblical?" Here's my brief answer: Even though you won't find the phrase "church membership" in the Bible, you'll most certainly find the concept, especially in Paul's first letter to the church at Corinth. For example, in 1 Corinthians 12 Paul refers to individual believers in the church as "parts" or "members of the body" at least *seventeen* times in order to teach them the necessity of humble interdependence. Further, in 1 Corinthians 14 Paul is concerned about "outsiders." He challenges the church to make sure "outsiders" are capable of understanding all that's said when they attend a gathering of "insiders"—a.k.a. a church service (14:23–25). On the other hand, in 1 Corinthians 5 Paul is concerned about "insiders." He commands the church to take someone who is currently "an insider" and make him "an outsider" (5:12–13). I'm not sure if the church at Corinth had a membership process exactly like the one in my congregation, but I'm certain that they had a process for determining who was an insider and who was an outsider. That's all church membership should be: a way of distinguishing insiders from "outsiders"—who's a member of the body, and who isn't?

In 1 Corinthians 5 Paul addressed a horrendous problem in the Corinthian congregation: The church was allowing a notoriously immoral man to remain an insider. It seems that this man was wealthy and influential. Apparently he had married a younger woman, then eventually entered an immoral relationship with her mother (who was probably closer to his age). Rather than grieving over the sin in their midst, some members in the church actually thought that their continued association with this man evidenced greater spiritual maturity (5:2)! Paul's goal in writing this chapter was to convince the church that they needed to make this insider an outsider. He repeatedly told them to remove him from membership (5:2, 5, 7, 11, 13). Paul offered three reasons for such drastic action.

The sinner's benefit (v. 5)—Because the man was acting like an unbeliever, Paul urged the church to treat him as such—not for his ultimate destruction, but for his ultimate salvation. "Excommunication" is meant to be *remedial, not terminal*. Churches practice it because they want those living in unrepentant sin to "be saved in the day of the Lord."

The church's purity (vv. 6-8)—Paul's thinking was soaked in Passover imagery. Jesus, the Passover Lamb, was sacrificed, so the church, like the Passover meal, should be free from yeast, a symbol of Israel's old way of life in Egypt. Notice how Paul reasons from *who you are* in Christ to *how you should live* as a Christian.

The church's witness (vv. 9-11)—Christians are not called to be *isolationists*—avoiding relationships with unbelieving sinners. Rather, Christians are called to be *evangelists*—testifying to unbelievers by our words and lives that the gospel saves us from sin.

Why is it so important to distinguish who's inside and who's outside the church? Because Christians are sheep whose lives should say, "I follow the Shepherd." Because Christians are new creations whose lives should say, "The old is gone; the new has come." The most basic responsiblitiy of church membership is living like a Christian. It's living out your profession—not perfectly, but consistently. It's obeying Christ, and repenting when you don't. Churches must *never* remove Christians from membership for sin—only for *unrepentant* sin.

I want to commit myself to a group of believers who takes our testimony for Christ so seriously that they're willing to dissociate with me if I live in unrepentant sin—if my walk doesn't match my talk. I want to be committed to a church that values my eternal good, our blood-bought purity, and the clarity of our witness to the unrepentant sinners we're seeking to reach. That's why I want to be a church member!

Let your testimony to the gospel's power and your burden for the gospel's advance be the reasons you're committed to church membership.—JOE

DAY 29 — READ ACTS 16

STRONG WOMEN MAKE STRONG CHURCHES

"And she prevailed upon us." ACTS 16:15

You may be thinking that the title has a typo. Don't I mean that "strong *men* make strong churches?" Well, yes, I concur with that notion. Local churches are indeed blessed to have strong men who are leading their families and the church as God has very clearly prescribed in Scripture. Godly men are essential to the well-being of the church. (See Joe's excellent article in *Gospel Meditations for Men*, Day 20.) But no, I didn't misspeak. Strong women make strong churches, too. Unfortunately, my experience is that some churches that rightly value men wrongly devalue women. Pastors, deacons, and even (especially?) other women are often threatened by ladies who have exceptional business savvy, leadership abilities, or insights into Scripture. Such thinking is small—and sinful. The Bible prohibits women from doing two very specific things in the church: *leading men and teaching men* (1 Timothy 2:12). We shouldn't omit those prohibitions as many are doing in our day. But neither should we amend them. Outside of teaching and leading men in the church, women can do a ton of good! In fact, they *have* when trusted and unfettered, ever since the book of Acts. Women prayed with the disciples in Acts 1. Women were among those persecuted for their faith in Acts 8–9. A woman hosted the church in her home in Acts 12. A demon-possessed girl was part of the church plant in Philippi in Acts 16. Three ladies are especially noted for their contributions to the church in the book of Acts:

Dorcas served the church as a minister of mercy (9:36–43). Dorcas is one of the "extras" in the drama in the book of Acts. She wasn't a star, by any means. But her untimely death left a gaping hole in her church. She was mourned as a "disciple" who was "full of good works and acts of charity" (v. 36). Apparently, she was especially attentive to the widows in the church, and they wept at her passing and spoke of her generosity and industry, showing the garments she had made for them (v. 39). Most likely, she was a single lady, and she embraced the opportunities it afforded. She wasn't waiting for life to begin. She was a vital member of a vibrant church.

Lydia served the church as a successful businesswoman and hostess (16:12–15, 40). Lydia is probably the counterpart to Dorcas. Whereas Dorcas appears to have had a relatively simple life, Lydia was a business tycoon. She was a merchant from Thyatira who was "a seller of purple goods" (v. 14). Though wealthy and religious, she was lost. When she heard the gospel from Paul, "the Lord opened her heart" (v. 14), and she and her household were among the first Europeans to trust Christ. Following her baptism, she insisted that Paul and Barnabas make her home their headquarters while in Philippi. She "urged" them and "prevailed" upon them (v. 15). That makes me smile. Paul, the fearless persuader, met his match in this spunky entrepreneur. Lydia didn't need to apologize for her business savvy as though it were unbecoming for a Christian woman. It's not! She was successful, and she leveraged her skills and assets to advance the gospel.

Priscilla served the church as a businesswoman, church planter, and teacher (Acts 18:1–28). Priscilla was a faithful wife, companion, and business partner for Aquilla. She is another woman of means who thrived as a hostess, both for Paul and later for a church that met in her home. She and her husband were mobile, and over a span of almost two decades they were involved in churches in Corinth (18:1–3), Ephesus (18:18–26), Rome (Romans 16:3–5), and again in Ephesus (2 Timothy 4:19). God used their "tent-making" for gospel advance, and he does the same today. Perhaps surprisingly, Priscilla was also a Bible teacher, and alongside her husband she instructed Apollos (Acts 18:24–28). Did she preach to men? I'm sure not. But she did explain the Bible to him, and he was secure and humble enough to take her superior knowledge as a blessing rather than a threat.

Ladies, be encouraged by these examples. Don't assume that ministry is for men. The church needs you—and not only in the nursery or kitchen! And men, don't be threatened by capable ladies. Lead them. But *unleash* them for the good of the church and the glory of Christ!

Let the gospel inspire you to maximize your skills and assets to strengthen the church.—CHRIS

DAY 30 — READ HEBREWS 12:1–11

ADDRESSED AS SONS

*"And have you forgotten the exhortation that addresses you as sons?
'My son, do not regard lightly the discipline of the Lord,
nor be weary when reproved by him.'"* HEBREWS 12:5

The use of the Old Testament Scriptures by the New Testament writers is a fascinating and complex subject. Though it is a difficult area of Bible interpretation, observing how the writers of the New Testament applied the Old Testament to their readers provides us with valuable spiritual insight into the importance and character of the Scriptures. Hebrews 12:5 is a good example.

Please notice these words: "Have you forgotten the exhortation that addresses you as sons?" These words are followed by a quotation from Proverbs 3:11–12. In its original Old Testament context, Solomon is offering instruction to his son about spiritual things. Here is what is striking—the writer of Hebrews tells his readers that the words of Solomon to his son were "address[ed to them] as sons." He personalizes the Old Testament text by making it a word from God to them. His direct, personal application of these ancient words is legitimate for two reasons.

Through inspiration, these words are God's words. The writer to the Hebrews can make this direct application to believers because of the inspiration of the Bible. The words of Scripture are God's Word communicated through human authors. In other words, Solomon's instruction to his son was at the same time God's instruction for his people. When the writer of Hebrews personalizes this Old Testament quotation, he is showing that he believes that Solomon's words were God's words. Another way in which the author of Hebrews does this is to quote the Old Testament and ascribe the quotation to the Holy Spirit (see, for example, Hebrews 3:7; 10:15). The underlying belief is clearly that the Old Testament is God's Word, not just the religious writings of men.

We can go beyond that to say that God superintended the writing of Scripture with a clear purpose in mind: to provide believers of all succeeding generations with all that is needed for life and godliness. Even though Solomon wrote the words almost 1,000 years before the writer of Hebrews quoted them, God had the needs of his people in mind when Solomon wrote them. God inspired and preserved them as a lasting exhortation for his people.

Through the gospel, we are God's children. The writer's application of the Old Testament to his readers is also legitimate because of the gospel—Jesus Christ provided the way for sinners to be reconciled to God. God can speak to us "as sons" because we have been adopted into his family. By virtue of our relationship to God through Jesus Christ, the Scriptures are full of promises, warnings, principles, and instruction for how we live as God's children.

What does this mean for the way that we handle the Bible? It should cause us to view the Bible as God's Word "addressed" to us as his children. That does not mean that we are careless about studying the context and proper application of the text. But it does mean that we should not treat the Bible as an archaic document that merely records historical facts, stories, and statements. Just as the writer of Hebrews could quote a 1,000-year-old text from Proverbs and say it was addressed to his readers, I believe we can say about all of the Bible, "God has spoken to us, let us hear him!"

Let the gospel control your view of the Scriptures so that you embrace them as a gracious gift from your Heavenly Father to guide your life and the church for his glory!—DAVE

DAY 31 — READ EPHESIANS 1 & 3:10, 20-21

TROPHIES OF GOD'S GRACE

"To the praise of his glory." EPHESIANS 1:12

A lot of ink has been spilled on the topic of the church's purpose in the world. *The church exists to attract the world. Or counteract the world. Or bring social justice to the world. Or provide a safe harbor from the world. Or....* You get the idea. However, the church's ultimate purpose doesn't relate to the world at all—or even to Christians. The church's primary purpose relates to God, not men. Whatever else we may accomplish in the world, our *raison d'être* is to bring glory to God. Ephesians, the quintessential book of the Bible on church doctrine and church life, makes this point early and often.

In Ephesians 1 Paul insists that the church exists for God's glory. The first three chapters of Ephesians are a beautiful description of the spiritual riches that have been lavished upon the church because of Christ Jesus. This "riches" language is repeated again and again (1:3, 7, 8, 11, 14, 18; 2:4, 7; 3:6, 8, 16). The premise of the whole book is given in Ephesians 1:3 where we are told to praise God for giving us "every spiritual blessing in Christ." This introduction is followed by three chapters of "show and tell" in which the inspired apostle, like a museum curator, takes us on a tour of the treasures of salvation. We have been chosen (1:4). We have been adopted (1:5). We have been redeemed and forgiven (1:7). We have been made heirs of an inheritance (1:11)—an inheritance guaranteed by the seal of the Spirit (1:14). We have been brought from spiritual death to spiritual life (2:1–10). We have been united to other Christians (2:11–22). We have been made recipients of "the unsearchable riches of Christ" (3:8). And on it goes. But *why*? Why has God taken spiritual corpses, given them spiritual life, then welcomed them as his spiritual children? The answer doesn't lie in us, but in God. God has saved us for himself, as Ephesians 1 reminds us three times:

- "To the praise of his glorious grace" (1:6).
- "So that we ... might be to the praise of his glory" (1:12).
- "To the praise of his glory" (1:14).

In Ephesians 3 Paul insists that the church exists for God's glory. The end of the doctrinal section of Ephesians doesn't come with a sigh but with a shout! Paul explains that the church is God's evidence to angels—*to angels!*—of his "manifold wisdom" (3:10). Paul crescendos through Chapter 3 until he finally uncorks with a glorious doxology:

> Now to him who is able to do far more abundantly than all that we ask or think, according to the power at work within us, to him be glory in the church and in Christ Jesus throughout all generations, forever and ever. Amen (3:20-21).

The church exists *by God's grace*. And the church exists *for God's glory*. Just as Colossians 1:16 says that all things were created "by him" and "for him," Ephesians teaches that *the church* exists "by him" and "for him." These truths should define us, direct us, and drive us. At Killian Hill Baptist Church, we summarize our responses to the gospel this way: *"Astonished by God's grace. Ambitious for God's glory."* That's why Jesus saved us, and preserves us, and uses us—for his glory. May we be ambitious to accomplish that high calling!

Holy, Mighty, Worthy, the first hymn Greg Habegger and I composed, climaxes with this great theme. I love to sing it with my own church family:

> "Glory, glory, glory!" We, Thy church, adore Thee.
> Called by grace to bring Thee praise; trophies of Thy pow'r to save!
> None shall share Thy glory! All shall bow before Thee.
> Father, Son and Spirit: One! "Glory, glory, glory!"

Let the gospel make your church passionate for God's glory.—CHRIS